THE ADHD
RESET

Quarto.com

© 2025 Quarto Publishing Group USA Inc.
Text © Claire Michalski

First Published in 2025 by Fair Winds Press, an imprint of The Quarto Group,
100 Cummings Center, Suite 265-D, Beverly, MA 01915, USA.
T (978) 282-9590 F (978) 283-2742

Fair Winds Press titles are also available at discount for retail, wholesale, promotional, and bulk
purchase. For details, contact the Special Sales Manager by email at specialsales@quarto.com or
by mail at The Quarto Group, Attn: Special Sales Manager, 100 Cummings Center, Suite 265-D,
Beverly, MA 01915, USA.

29 28 27 26 25   1 2 3 4 5

ISBN: 978-0-7603-9127-3

Digital edition published in 2025
eISBN: 978-0-7603-9128-0

Library of Congress Cataloging-in-Publication Data available

Design: Samantha J. Bednarek, samanthabednarek.com
Illustration: Mattie Wells Design

Printed in China

The information in this book is for educational purposes only. It is not intended to replace the advice
of a physician or medical practitioner. Please see your health-care provider before beginning any
new health program.

THE ADHD RESET

Shift Your Mindset.
Find Clarity.
Unlock Your Magic.

CLAIRE MICHALSKI
Creator of @ModernHippieMindset

FAIR WINDS

CONTENTS

Your Past

Your Present

Your Future

INTRODUCTION

THE ADHD RESET will take you on the ultimate self-discovery journey. This is the *exact* journey I had to take myself. This book is designed to help you not just navigate attention deficit hyperactivity disorder (ADHD) but also use your unique qualities to totally own and enjoy life with it!

Without the right tools, ADHD can rule your life in a challenging way. But I'm here to guide you through all the ways in which you can make ADHD work for you. While you can't change the fact that you have ADHD—I know, it's a lifelong dealio—you *can* reset your mindset and approach to living with ADHD!

This book is like having me as a personal cheerleader and coach in one. I'll teach you the right steps to take, the changes to make, and the new ways to pick yourself up if you fall. As you go through this journey as I have mapped out in the pages to come, you will realize, as I did, that ADHD makes you one of the most magical people on the planet!

Your Magical ADHD Brain

People with ADHD are magical because ADHD brains are essentially right-brain biased. The right side of our brain is in charge of things such as imagination, creativity, intuition, holistic thinking, nonverbal communication, feelings, rhythm, and visualization! In fact, the right side of our brain contains all the magical parts that make us what we are!

So, we're going to home in on exactly this and put our focus toward the positive symptoms of ADHD that enable us to multitask, adapt to new situations, hyperfocus, be resilient, have lots of energy, and more. I'll show you that each positive ADHD trait can be harnessed, nurtured, and applied so you can create your dream life!

Accepting Yourself as You Are

We aren't going to shy away from the difficulties faced by those with ADHD, and you will have plenty of aha moments as you see yourself in these pages. But you will be empowered to lovingly accept those parts of yourself through shadow work, reframing techniques, subconscious rewiring, and more.

These are all methodologies I have studied and applied to become the person I am today.

A person whom I love.

If you knew the negative way I used to speak about myself, you'd know just how remarkable it is that I now openly embrace self-love! Now I use the methods outlined in this book to guide clients to help them reach their fullest potential.

Transform Your Outlook

Your reset will transform your outlook on your life: past, present, and future. It's important for us to reflect and heal before we move to the now and beyond! After learning exactly how to truly love yourself, rebuild your self-trust, and enhance your confidence, your ADHD reset will give you a newfound excitement and belief in yourself to pursue your wildest dreams!

You'll shift from a fixed mindset to a growth mindset and add some much-needed sparkle back into your life by exploring the more logical and less woo-woo side of manifestation!

The words "You have lost the sparkle in your eyes" still echo in my mind. They were spoken by a dear friend who noticed the gradual fading of my sparkly zest for life, replaced by anger, frustration, and a general sense of misery. So, I know what it's like to feel lifeless. But I also know what it's like to add that fairy-dust feeling back into your being!

Change Your Mindset

I want to give you your wings back—I have dedicated my life to liberating people from the confines of their own mental birdcages. By the end of this transformation, you will not just feel magical . . . you will be free!

The mindset reset practices we will focus on will free you from limiting beliefs, negative self-talk, self-sabotage, unhealthy habits, chaotic emotions, and much more. You are about to go from feeling limited to limitless!

I used to feel very limited in life, and the thing about feeling something is that you *become* the exact thing you feel. So, I *was* limited. I was limiting myself. I had blocked the magic I used to hold within as a child—the belief that I could make a difference in the world. I hid exactly what made me stand out!

My Journey to Self-Love

My journey to becoming the woman that I love today feels like the world's longest and somewhat loneliest research study. I chose to get a private diagnosis to avoid the lengthy National Health Service (NHS) waitlist in the UK. The problem I faced after diagnosis was learning that I would have to continue expensive private care to get any ADHD treatment. The UK's NHS will not always transfer the care.

So after being somewhat abandoned by the system after diagnosis, I tried anything I heard about that promised to make me a "better human": better functioning, better focused, better committed, better moods, better at simply being—at existing!

It wasn't until my ADHD diagnosis that I realized many of the things I had implemented would need tweaking to better suit a neurodivergent mind. The ways I had been trying to help myself were all neurotypical healing and coping techniques. I needed to dive much deeper into the way my brain works!

Since then, I've taken the results of my one-person study and applied it to helping my clients as well as hundreds of thousands of others across the world through social media. Now it's time for *you* to go through the ADHD Reset.

I'm with you every step of the way. *Let's do this!*

How to Read This Book

Let's address the elephant in the room—that is, being easily distracted and losing focus, which makes it difficult to finish things, such as this book!

In this instance, it is ADHD itself that can be the obstacle! I'll admit that even I find reading somewhat boring at times. So, how have I managed to not only read a house full of books but written one too? I make things easy for myself! We need to make this commitment as easy as possible for you too!

How to Get Started and Keep Reading

If you tend to avoid reading or find it challenging, I recommend committing to just ten minutes per day. At this steady pace, you will average around five pages a day and finish the book within two months.

From just ten little minutes a day for a couple of months, you can achieve a total transformation!

To kick-start this small daily commitment, pick a time that best suits you to read, then set up a daily reminder on your phone. When this reminder goes off, use this as your trigger to put your phone on Do Not Disturb. In fact, it's probably a good idea to title the reminder something like "Do not disturb, I'm reading!" Fun, relevant, and encouraging emojis are always welcome too, of course!

I like using my timer when I make a reading commitment. The timer always goes off way sooner than I expect it to, and I often end up reading for longer and feel really good about myself.

→ WRITE IT DOWN: List Your Obstacles and Find Solutions

Grab your journal and write down a list of the things that could prevent you from completing *The ADHD Reset*. For instance:

- Scrolling on my phone instead of reading
- Missing a day of reading and then not going back to it
- Being distracted by phone notifications

Once you have written down your list of possible obstacles, write down a list of solutions. Below are some examples for inspiration, but please adapt them to be your own, and be as detailed as possible. Finding your *own* solutions increases the likelihood of success for you! Adding detail gives you a realistic viewpoint of the action you are intending to take. Here are some strategies I use:

- **Scrolling on my phone instead of reading:** I will set a daily repeated alarm for 9:00 p.m. with the title "Change your life instead of scrolling!" because I often don't realize what the time is and lose hours on my phone at night.
- **Missing a day of reading and then not going back to it:** I am going to commit to reading four evenings a week for twenty minutes because then if I miss a night, I have more flexibility and don't feel pressured to read every day! I'll make a checklist in my notes so I get a hit of dopamine when I check it off each time.
- **Being distracted by phone notifications:** When reading, I am going to put my phone on Do Not Disturb mode so that I don't get any notifications.

- Change the background of your phone to a picture of the book so that when you reach for your phone to do some doom scrolling, you are reminded that you could read *The ADHD Reset* instead and change your life!
- Place the book where you intend to read, such as your bedside table.
- Charge your phone away from your bed to reduce distraction for evening reading.
- Set reading reminders with an encouraging alarm title, such as "Just ten minutes to change my life."
- Reduce and adjust your commitment to a single page or just five minutes of reading if you are feeling overwhelmed on certain days. This often results in you doing more than you intended to and helps regulate your mood!
- Treat yourself as you read. You could have a hot drink, put on a face mask, light some candles. Make it feel exactly like what it is: self-care!

How to Make This Book Work for You

This isn't an ordinary book—it's like having an ADHD coach, and each ten minutes of daily reading is your private coaching session. So, it's important to be honest with yourself throughout your journey in order to get the most out of these transformative mindset practices.

What You Need to Complete Your ADHD Reset

Pen and Paper

I recommend having a designated journal or notepad to use alongside this book. This will act as your private and safe space to share, learn, heal, and grow. It doesn't have to be anything fancy! I want you to feel free to pour your thoughts onto the pages of your journal—scribble, cross things out, circle, underline, whatever you want! It's your space to grow, and growth can sometimes look messy!

Honesty

Throughout your ADHD reset, it is important for you to be honest with yourself. This is how you are going to get the most out of the upcoming transformative mindset practices. Within these pages and your journal, you are safe to be yourself, ditch the ego, and be free from judgment. "I'm fine" never sparks positive changes.

Make a Commitment to Yourself

Most importantly, I need your commitment to see this through. I'm not going to trick you into thinking that this will be an easy-breezy journey, but it does require you to make just one single commitment: finish the book. There is no rush. You are not in a race. You can take your time at whatever pace feels right to you regardless of my reading recommendation. This is your journey. Take it one page at a time, but make the nonnegotiable commitment to finish the book. You'll find more about how to do this in the next section. I know it won't always be easy for you to open the pages of this book, put pen to paper, and avoid the quick-fix dopamine hits of social media and the like, but your commitment to keep returning to these pages is you returning to yourself—the person whom you can become! Together we'll navigate the challenges and celebrate the victories, knowing that each effort brings you closer to unlocking your full potential and the magic within!

Make Your Own Commitment *Now*

To cement this commitment, tell people about it. Tell loved ones, post it on social media, say loud and proud:

> I am committed to reading this book and transforming my life!

→ WRITE IT DOWN: I Am Committed

Now that you've committed to reading this book and have learned ways to overcome obstacles and complete it, write down *why* you are going to do this. Be detailed. Give yourself a sense of the reward you will get and reconfirm your commitment. For example:

> **I am committed to reading *The ADHD Reset* because** . . . I am tired of feeling like I don't have control over my life. I see others with ADHD who are thriving, and I want to thrive too! This one single commitment is going to take me on a transformative journey, and I can't wait to get to the end of the book and feel confident, happier, excited about life, and better regulated—to just feel better about myself overall! I am committed.

My Commitment to You

I am committed to helping as many people as possible. It is my life calling, and through the magic of manifestation (I'll spill the tea on that later), I am able to reach more people through the pages of this book. I decided early on in the writing process that I wanted this book to feel like I am there with you through each step that you take. I want to be transparent about my struggles and how I overcame them and to make you feel less alone. My commitment is to be there for you throughout this journey.

We are all on different paths, but I know that we will have all started our ADHD journey with one big question: "Do I have ADHD?"

The *Big* Question:
Do I Have ADHD?

"DO I HAVE ADHD?" You've probably asked yourself this question—maybe more than once.

It feels like such a Big Question, one that comes with a mixture of fear, anxiety, and overwhelm, but also hope and often a huge sense of relief! Before you ask yourself the Big Question, "Do I have ADHD?," what you have secretly and repeatedly asked yourself many times throughout your life is much more unsettling. "What is wrong with me?!"

And *this* question doesn't come with any hope or sense of relief. It's just a looming, unanswered query that we have all had creeping around our minds while living with undiagnosed ADHD. So, I'm going to answer that ever-looming, lifelong question—What is wrong with you?—right now. Absolutely nothing!

It's not a matter of anything being *wrong*; rather, it's about recognizing that you simply don't fit the standard mold. You are a neuro-spicy square peg trying to fit yourself into a boring round hole!

But I get it—your world has been a constant trigger for you to question your capabilities, your intelligence, and even your sanity! Your confidence has understandably been dam-aged along the way, and your subconscious mind absolutely needs more evidence to *truly* believe that there is nothing wrong with you. I am going to give your subconscious mind all the evidence it needs throughout *The ADHD Reset*.

So many of us doubt our gut instinct when we are first learning about ADHD. We flick constantly between "Do I?" and "Don't I?" and often put off getting answers out of fear of judgment.

The Undiagnosed ADHD Experience

Living with undiagnosed ADHD begins with you questioning from a young age why you feel different. You feel quite magical as a child with a more-vivid-than-average imagination and a never-ending supply of energy, but you also notice that you feel things much more intensely than those around you.

You also pick up on exactly how other people feel even when they don't share it. As you are developing your ADHD mask (more about this in chapter 3) to hide your expressive emotions and big feelings, everyone else is totally unmasked to you. You can see, hear, and feel all facial expressions, body language, tones of voice, and energy. You notice what others don't. After all, ADHD isn't really having an attention deficit. Instead, it's paying attention to too much, in too much detail, *all the time*. You become hyperaware as a result and can often feel responsible for how others feel simply because you seem to be the only one that notices.

This is when people-pleasing begins. You are full of energy, but sometimes it's considered too much, so you tone that down. You love to learn but struggle to learn in the way the grown-ups want you to. Sitting still in a classroom doesn't scratch the excitement-craving itch that you have. Your body becomes restless, and your mind wanders from the lesson toward an inner self-made adventure.

As you grow older and try out new things that you inevitably become quickly bored with, you begin to feel like the person who gives up, and the limiting belief of "I am a failure" sets in place. This makes you feel insecure.

You aren't sure of what path to take as each chapter of life unfolds. There are so many options, yet they simultaneously feel like an abundance of exciting opportunities and a bunch of pointless endeavors that will ultimately defeat you.

To give your brain the *guaranteed* dopamine reward that your educational and career choices can't always provide, you begin to turn to unhealthy habits such as smoking, drinking, phone scrolling, excessive gaming, binge eating, out-of-control shopping, and so on. You may also seek stimulating situations that give you spikey shots of cortisol, such as unhealthy relationships, scary movies, gossip, arguments, and even lawbreaking!

As life becomes a long list of to-dos, must-dos, and absolutely-have-to-dos to survive, you once again feel like the child in the classroom: you know that you can do it but you aren't sure exactly how. Stress, anxiety, and a general sense of overwhelm become a cemented part of your daily life, and you are never fully rested or emotionally regulated. This results in you often questioning your sanity and reaching out for help but being told you have anxiety, depression, or stress. Then one life-changing day, you see or hear the list of ADHD symptoms and finally ask the Big Question, "Do I have ADHD?"

Struggling with ADHD Symptoms

While everyone's journey is unique, there are some things I would happily place a bet on, and I'm not a gambling girl! Unless diagnosed at a young age, you have been searching for answers and self-analyzing for as long as you can remember.

You have been struggling with symptoms for years. However, all these symptoms are so easily brushed off, pushed into another diagnosis by medical professionals and others. This can result in you turning against yourself, like I did, with damaging messages such as:

Procrastination: "I'm so lazy."
Binge eating: "I'm unhealthy and lazy."
Quitting things before completion: "F*ck me, Claire, why are you so lazy?!"
Depressive episodes: "Okay, maybe I have depression?"
Mood swings: "Or perhaps bipolar?"
Angry outbursts: "Yep. Bipolar."
Bad memory: "I'm an idiot."
Bad grades at school because you struggle to learn through listening to lectures: "Definitely an idiot!"
Getting told off for disrupting others, talking too much, and not paying attention: "An idiot with a class-clown flare."
Easily overwhelmed by tasks that involve . . . anything with structure: "I can't cope with life. Something is wrong with me."
Perceiving constructive criticism as an *actual threat*: "I'm too sensitive."
Breaking down in tears if anything is rejection related: "I'm far too sensitive!"
Overthinking everything: "FFS, can I please just chill out?!"
Believing everyone hates you: "Get a grip."
Feeling like a failure: "Because I am one."

You are not your unmanaged symptoms. Your symptoms are simply unmanaged.

It's clear to see how easily we can gaslight ourselves and turn the things we have struggled with into sources of shame and "proof" of simply sucking! Others may have misdiagnosed you:

A teacher says to you: "You lack concentration."
A teacher tells your parents: "She's in her own world."
Your partner proclaims: "You're too much sometimes."
A friend jokes: "You're batshit crazy!"
An employer encouragingly suggests: "You're not living up to your full potential."
(That one hurt.)

It's an accumulation of these surface-level explanations for your way of being that slowly but absolutely results in low self-worth and a total absence of belief in yourself.

ADHD 101: Gaslighting

Having ADHD can make you doubt yourself.
This can lead to gaslighting by others and even self-gaslighting.

Gaslighting
This is a form of manipulation where someone tries to make another person doubt their own thoughts, feelings, and reality.

Self-Gaslighting
Self-gaslighting happens when you doubt yourself or invalidate your own reality and lived experiences.

Examples of Self-Gaslighting
- Questioning your own memory or perception of events
- Minimizing your own feelings and emotions
- Blaming yourself for someone else's negative behavior
- Ignoring red flags or gut instincts
- Doubting your abilities or your own worth

Diagnosed versus Undiagnosed ADHD

If you are living with the scary Big Question—"Do I have ADHD?"—right now, let me make this moment much more manageable for you.

First, decide if you need a formal diagnosis. I advocate getting a diagnosis if you can. It's not about the label, and most definitely not to make excuses, but rather to make sense of your past and validate your lived experience. Plus, if you're anything like me, you probably don't like having unanswered questions rolling around in your mind! But it's a personal choice. It seems that for as many of us who feel the need to formally and officially be told we have ADHD, there is a huge undiagnosed ADHD community.

Not everyone feels that it's necessary to have it confirmed. Maybe impatience with the diagnostic process, waitlists, and being afraid to raise issues with your doctor comes into play here too.

ADHD: Keeping It Simple

The Pros and Cons of Being Undiagnosed

PROS of remaining undiagnosed	CONS of remaining undiagnosed
You are free of labels.	You can't easily explain symptoms.
You remain free of the associated stigma.	You live with uncertainty.
You rely on personal coping strategies.	You may lack professional support.
You avoid potentially slipping into the victim mindset.	You don't come to terms with all the ways that ADHD has impacted your life.

→ WRITE IT DOWN: Explore Your Feelings about Being Diagnosed or Undiagnosed

Whether you are diagnosed or undiagnosed, grab your journal and write on a page "Why do I need to know?" or "Why *did* I need to know?" Then spell out why you feel you need or needed this answer.

For those already diagnosed, the following journal prompts act as an important reflective practice to become more mindful of your journey so far. You'll find **undiagnosed** and **diagnosed** versions of each question.

Six Questions to Ask Yourself Pre- and Post-ADHD Diagnosis

If you're undiagnosed, when asking the first two questions below, consider if having a professional diagnosis will bring you clarity and peace or if you can validate your lived experience yourself. If you've been diagnosed, reflect on how this validation felt to you and whether this has had a positive or negative effect on your self-esteem.

1. **Undiagnosed:** Will a diagnosis validate my lived experience?
   Diagnosed: Did the diagnosis make sense of my lived experience? If so, how?

2. **Undiagnosed:** Why do I need this validation?
   Diagnosed: Did it feel valuable to unpack my past from this new perspective of having ADHD?

There is no right answer to the following question (or to any of the questions, in fact). Question 3 is to prompt you to be mindful of your mindset and to prepare you for the potential of mixed emotions. For the diagnosed, this question prompts you to reflect on the emotions that you may have not yet processed after getting an ADHD diagnosis— because it's kind of a big deal!

3. **Undiagnosed:** Will a diagnosis feel like a relief, like a new hurdle, or both?
   Diagnosed: Did the diagnosis bring me relief, pose new challenges, or perhaps a combination of both?

For question 4, think about what knowing will not only mean to you but also how it will positively change your life if you believe it will. Knowledge is power but only if you use it positively! My diagnosis most definitely changed my life in amazing ways, but only because I perceived the diagnosis as a relief and the beginning of a positive and freeing journey. For those diagnosed, reflect on what you have done with this knowledge. Have you used it in a positive way in your life so far?

4. **Undiagnosed:** What will I do with knowing I have ADHD?
Diagnosed: What has the knowledge of having ADHD meant for me?

What Is the Victim Mindset?

Before you answer question 5, you need to know what the "victim mindset" is.

A victim mindset is when a person lives in *effect* of their own life. Things happen *to* them instead of *for* them. An example of the victim mindset is when someone moans about a negative situation in their life but does nothing to change it. The victim mindset is very easy to slip into!

The victim mindset can show up in smaller ways in our day-to-day lives. For instance, someone gets stuck in traffic each morning. They get stressed, they curse, they huff and puff, but they never adjust their route or the time that they leave their house. Then they show up to work late, express their stress to a colleague, huff and puff some more, and *then* start their day feeling like the world is once again against them.

There is no shame in having a victim mindset. I have been here. I was very much this person for a long period of time. I felt like a total victim to my circumstances. If I had gotten my diagnosis then, with *that* mindset, I think it would have sunk me. I would have unconsciously used ADHD as another reason for my woes. I would have used it to excuse every negative behavior, every misfortune, and every perceived failing. I would have leaned into it as a victimized identity. This is why it's best to adopt a growth mindset before getting your diagnosis. (Developing a growth mindset after your diagnosis is life changing too!)

Moving toward a Growth Mindset

Knowing the reason why you want the diagnosis is extremely important. A diagnosis will always be a lot to process and comes with many emotions, but it should be uplifting and empowering! By answering these questions, it gently nudges you toward a growth mindset, pre-and post-diagnosis.

5. **Undiagnosed:** Will having a diagnosis confirmed empower me, or will it push me into a victim mindset?
Diagnosed: Did receiving my diagnosis empower me, or has it made me become reliant on the label and fall into the victim mindset?

If you recognize that diagnosis triggers a victim mindset, write down all the reasons why getting a diagnosis benefits and empowers you!

ADHD: Keeping It Simple

Victim Mindset versus Growth Mindset

Victim Mindset

The victim mindset is a belief system where you perceive yourself as powerless and blame external factors for your circumstances.

Do You . . .

- Blame others or circumstances for your problems?
- Feel helpless or lack energy?
- Seek sympathy and external validation?
- Avoid responsibility and accountability?
- View challenges as impossible obstacles that will defeat you?
- Resist change?
- Refuse solution-based suggestions?
- Lack personal growth?

Growth Mindset

The growth mindset is a belief system where you perceive challenges as opportunities for growth and embrace effort and perseverance to achieve success.

Do You . . .

- Embrace challenges as opportunities for learning and development?
- Demonstrate persistence and resilience in the face of setbacks?
- Believe in the power of effort to achieve goals?
- Feel open to feedback and constructive criticism?
- View criticism as an opportunity to learn and improve?
- Inspire others with a positive attitude and commitment to personal growth?

Taking Meds or Not?

Another aspect of deciding if you would like to get a diagnosis is medication.

6. **Undiagnosed:** Will I consider medication once I am diagnosed?
   Diagnosed: Did I consider medication? Am I on medication? How has it been? Would I like to remain on it?

If you do decide to get diagnosed, whether or not to take medication is a very personal choice. You'll want to discuss taking medication for ADHD with your health-care practitioner.

Full transparency, I am not medicated. However, I do self-manage symptoms and regularly take supplements. My proactive approach to ADHD management means I live a very happy and successful life without medication.

For example, it takes someone with focus, energy, and time management skills to write a book and get it published. These are all traits ADHDers are deemed not to have, yet here you are reading the words about how to live a successful life with ADHD from a diagnosed, unmedicated ADHDer herself.

There *are* health issues that quite literally need medication to survive. ADHD is one of them for many people, because ADHD without support (such as *The ADHD Reset*), symptom management, and/or medication can be life-threatening.

My Diagnosis

I got a private diagnosis to avoid a three-year waitlist via the UK's National Health Service. Once I had paid for my diagnosis, I wrongly assumed I could transfer my care back to the NHS. Wrong! In order for me to receive medication, I had to be diagnosed through their system, meaning I had to pay for medication privately or start the entire process again and wait three-plus years for a diagnosis I already had!

At the time, I couldn't afford to buy the ADHD medication privately. So, this left me with no option but to explore alternate solutions for the duration of the waitlist or until I could afford to pay, whichever came first! I felt so abandoned and unsupported that, after being diagnosed, I became quite angry. I would often think, "What good is a diagnosis to me if no one is going to help?!"

How wrong I was. I now view the systematic abandonment as a twisted turn of fate! I was left hopelessly unmedicated, which forced me to begin trying to ease my symptoms with mindset practices, lifestyle choices, management tools, and a sh*t ton of persistence through every trial-and-error attempt I made.

This is why I am here today. It's kind of like when you have a breakup glow-up! Initially you feel heartbroken, as though you will never be able to live without them. Then something remarkable happens: you pick yourself up and become even better than before! I guess having the traditional health-care system break up with me was my glow-up moment!

I could have so easily slipped into the victim mindset once again, but I actively chose growth, and I will get you to do this too! The victim mindset feels like the easy option because we are leaning into excuses, avoiding responsibility, seeking comforting sympathy, maintaining familiarity, and avoiding change. However, all those "easy options" are exactly what create a difficult life. It keeps us stuck feeling miserable, never progressing, and having a life that may not make us happy! I heard the saying "Choose your hard" one time, and that really stuck with me.

The victim mindset offers *temporary* relief only. The growth mindset may seem like the more difficult option because it requires effort—choose your hard! You'll need to shift criticism into moments of learning, reframe challenges into opportunities for growth, and embrace change. The long-term benefits far outweigh the short-term resistance. Your life *will* become easier! The fact that you're here now is proof that you are ready for this change.

Change always begins with self-reflection. Without reflecting you cannot become aware of what exactly you would like to change. Now that you've answered the questions in this chapter, you have taken the first step of your journey.

→ REFLECT AND ACT: Self Exploration and Growth

Read over and reflect on the answers you gave to the questions in this chapter. Question if your answers reflect you being in a victim mindset or a growth mindset. Be kind to yourself! Whatever your answers are and whichever mindset you feel you fit into currently, you are acting from a growth mindset while reading this book!

The Most Important Things You Need to Know

- Self-gaslighting happens when you doubt yourself or invalidate your reality and lived experiences.
- You get to choose if your diagnosis triggers growth or victimization within you.
- A growth mindset can be adopted at any time in your life.
- Choose your hard! The growth mindset feels difficult, but so does having a victim mindset!

Listen to Your Intuition:
Why You Need to Ask "Why?"

I HAVE A HANDY HABIT OF ASKING, "WHY?" It's a habit I want you to adopt too, or perhaps I should say *readopt*. It's a simple and common question that we need to include in our thoughts and conversations. Asking why helps us tap into the power of our intuition, our inner knowing, but we often swallow this word and stop seeking answers.

Why We Stop Asking "Why?"

Most ADHD children are extremely curious and tend to be the kids who accidentally get on our parents' last nerve by repeatedly asking, "Why is this? Why is that? But why???" We want all the answers. We love to fully understand things and, regardless of our grades at school, we love learning!

However, as we carried this curious nature from our homelife into our school life, we hit a big obstacle. Asking why can make us feel vulnerable! We did not want it to be obvious that we didn't catch the instructions or understand the task in class (that everyone else was already scribbling down as fast as lightning!).

We simply wanted to fit in and not have our intelligence questioned or be compared to our peers. Our curiosity doesn't waver as we grow older, nor does our gut instinct that triggers us to wonder about something. But after repetitive negative associations to asking why, acting on it certainly diminishes.

Asking Why Helped Me Find Answers

Luckily for me, my dad encouraged me to constantly ask why when it came to anything health related. My dad had some ongoing issues and fought for answers to get to good health. His ADHD had been overlooked, like for many others, and his symptoms had been attributed to his thyroid condition.

So, when a doctor told me, "You have depression," I was triggered to simply ask why. I was often met with the explanation that "depression is a disease," a "chemical imbalance" that is out of our control. Call it stubbornness, but I wasn't very welcoming of these explanations. In fact, it just made me once again ask, "Why? Why do I have a chemical imbalance? How do you know? You haven't tested anything. Why does this happen? What's causing it? Why?" To begin trusting your intuition, I'd like you to begin paying attention to your curious nature. In this chapter I'll also show you ways to regain the power of your intuition by including it in your thinking and the words you use.

→ WRITE IT DOWN: Tap into Your Curiosity

Every feeling has a physical sensation. It's important to pay attention to how you feel. In your journal, write "I am curious . . . ," then jot down a few things you feel curious about. Perhaps it's a topic you're interested in learning more about. Maybe you'd like to know the real reason Britney Spears dances in front of the entire world like nobody's watching, or what's going to happen in the next episode of your recent Netflix binge.

Once you have a curious list, read them to yourself and notice how you feel. As you do, ask yourself these questions:

- Does the feeling have movement or is it still?
- Does the feeling have any temperature?
- Does the feeling have color when you think about it?
- Does the feeling appear as a shape?

I feel curiosity as a triangle from my stomach, through my chest, and up to the front of my head. It has movement and feels like my stomach sends intuitive signals.

We'll work more on identifying different feelings in this book, but consider this as the start of your "How My Feelings Feel" list. For now, just write down whatever comes up when you feel curious. How does it feel for you?

This is important because this feeling helps you identify when you need more information or clarification. So, it's a good time to ask why. Later in the book I'll help you identify other important feelings so that you can more easily tell them apart and understand what your body is trying to tell you.

Learning to Listen to Your Intuition

Being in a doctor's office can be daunting. We sense our doctor's authority and often ignore our own senses because of it—you know, like when you feel like you aren't being heard, or you leave their office with an answer that you know doesn't solve the problem you arrived with. For this reason, a typical doctor's office visit is a good way to illustrate why it's important to listen to your intuition and use the power of asking why.

The first "Why?" you ask needs to be an internal question: "Why do I feel uneasy?" or perhaps "Why am I feeling curious?" This is you taking an interest in what you are sensing in the moment instead of ignoring it! You are becoming curious about your intuition. Asking why is your intuition's best friend!

Once you question things, you'll receive an answer from your intuition, just as I did when I thought, "A diagnosis of depression doesn't give me the full picture." Exploring your intuition is an act of self-validation. You tap into your intuition by asking yourself why you're feeling a certain way, then you listen for the answer and act on this "knowing."

The next "Why?" needs to be outwardly spoken and directed at whoever can give you the answer you need. In this scenario, it's your doctor. They may be somewhat surprised that you are looking for a more thorough explanation than what they have already given. However, in my experience, asking why often results in a friendly back-and-forth conversation where I feel more heard and taken seriously.

The few doctors whose feathers are ruffled by your inquisitive nature may not always give you answers as their egos spike, but it doesn't matter. Once you have listened to your intuition and asked the question, you are much more likely to find the answers for yourself.

This is so helpful when it comes to decision-making! Tapping into your intuition by asking why can help you navigate a diagnosis journey, such as deciding if you want to try certain medications or different management tools. Even day-to-day decisions are made easier. I often use this technique when I intuitively feel resistance to something or someone! I ask why and I never fail to give myself or find an answer.

ADHD: Keeping It Simple

Use the Power of Why with Doctors

Most people with ADHD are very curious and inquisitive. But when you feel the need to mask or cover up your true self, especially with authority figures like doctors, your curiosity can be suppressed. Here are a few subtle and polite approaches to kick-start your curious dialogue without stepping on anyone's toes!

- "You are the expert, so I'd like to ask you why . . ."
- "Thank you for everything you have explained to me so far. I really appreciate tapping into your knowledge. Could you explain X a little more so I understand why?"
- "I understand X but I'm struggling to make sense of Y. You're the best person to ask! Can you make it clear for me?"
- "Thank you. That makes sense, but X still doesn't. I'm wondering why . . ."
- "Thanks for that. I really like to have a full understanding, but I'm not sure why . . ."

Once you feel more confident, you can be more direct. For example:

- "Could you clarify why you made this decision?"
- "Would you mind explaining why you chose this approach?"
- "Could you walk me through your thinking behind this?"
- "I'm trying to understand your perspective. Would you be willing to explain it?"
- "Why?"

In all life scenarios, the more you know, the better. As the old saying goes, knowledge is power.

Is It Just Depression or Is It ADHD?

It's not surprising that I was given a diagnosis of depression prior to receiving the ADHD evaluation. It happens often within our community. I'm sure many of you will have also sat opposite a doctor and been given this or a similar explanation for your ongoing concerns.

In fact, CHADD (Children and Adults with Attention-Deficit/Hyperactivity Disorder), an organization dedicated to providing evidence-based information, shared that "some experts claim that up to 70 percent of those with ADHD will be treated for depression at some point in their lives." It's often referred to as a common comorbid or coexisting condition. Somehow I felt in my gut that depression was coexisting with something else undiscovered.

Instinctively I knew that the "depression" was part of something else, not *the* stand-alone thing! Perhaps it was denial, maybe an absolute stubbornness I seem to be plagued with, or my magical intuition, but I was not particularly accepting when my doctor only wanted to provide medication for simply being blue.

Finding the Missing Puzzle Piece

Without anyone knowing, for years I curiously researched all types of depression symptoms, and I didn't feel I was a perfect fit. You know, because of the glaringly obvious ADHD I have! Depression felt more like one of those puzzle pieces that kind of fits in place but I had to smoosh it in. You outright *know* it's *not* the piece that you're looking for, but it can live there until the actual missing puzzle piece turns up and fits in perfectly.

I eventually and reluctantly accepted aid for depression, but I still had that very niggling feeling of "There's something more to this—I know it!"

When we sense something doesn't feel quite right, or when our curiosity is triggered, this is our intuition screaming out to us, pleading with us to listen to what it has pieced together; take action, avoid something, investigate further!

Listen to Intuition, Ask Questions, Get Answers

When we learn to actively listen to our intuition and notice our curiosity, we know when to ask why. This is something that an intuitive neuroscientist does when they investigate exactly what depression is. Which just goes to show how clever it is to ask that little question!

Asking why I may or may not have depression led me to discover the neuroscientist Dr. Caroline Leaf. She explains that the "depression is a disease" statement is in fact a theory. It's a strong theory, but it simply isn't fact.

ADHD MAGIC! Your Intuition

Intuition is defined differently by each person you speak to! Some describe it as a feeling they get without conscious thought. Others say it is a spiritual gift. Neuroscience explains it as a complex process that involves neural connections, conscious thinking, and subconscious thinking! Everyone I know with ADHD seems to have this unconscious spiritual neurosciency gift, so I dug around to find why this could be.

Andrew Lewis, the founder of the ADHD coaching and resource website SimplyWellbeing, thinks he may have cracked the neurological code. He explains that those with ADHD rely more on the nonverbal workings of the interconnected right brain, and we have a right-brain bias!

The human brain has two main parts: the right brain and the left brain. The right side of an ADHD brain is stronger than the left due to poor dopamine connectivity. This means our right brain becomes dominant. The right brain is all about feelings, creativity, and seeing connections—the big picture!

With ADHD, when we learn or see something new, our brains try to fit it in with all the other information we already know. We make quick connections!

Research shows that ADHD adults can process more external information than average due to the right-brain bias. This means we also receive quicker feedback and have intuitive feelings more often than our neurotypical friends who may not absorb as much.

But I also like the explanation: we are witchy, wizardy, intuitive, super-magical ADHDers!

You can pick which explains your magic best!

Depression is commonly described as having a chemical imbalance that is out of our control and often unmeasurable. If you've struggled with depressive periods for a long time, learning that this is theoretical is hard to hear from your doctor or anyone else.

Heck, this is what my mom has been telling me all my life! For years, she encouraged me to take antidepressants because "you're like your dad; it's a chemical imbalance and sometimes you need medicine." At the time, I would look at my dad and think, "Does he struggle with depression? Why don't I feel like that fits with what I'm seeing?"

Yes, he got stressed and overwhelmed often, and he had to take naps because he often felt both mentally and physically exhausted. But the man built a successful business from scratch. He worked his ass off every day since his first job as a young child picking potatoes out of the countryside fields during the summer holidays. My dad is a go-getter! He makes sh*t happen! At just twenty years old, he crawled out of the literal mining pit he was working in and created a life where, even now as a retiree, he casually makes passive income while sitting on a beach somewhere warm.

The depression diagnosis just didn't fit. I thought, "You know what? I don't think he struggles with depression. I think the man is managing a busy business from an extra-busy brain just like my own, and it feels like a daily struggle to do that." I know—you are all wondering or probably yelling from your mind, "Your dad has ADHD!"

Now in retirement, he is staying comfortably in the undiagnosed ADHD community. He's no longer a businessperson juggling a wide range of hobbies or obligations as an extra-energetic parent to three young kids. He now blissfully enjoys the fruits of his labor—being energetic with grown-up kids and a few less new hobbies.

I know my mom was being supportive during those periods of woe and relaying information she trusted from health professionals who thought they were right, and perhaps still do! There is no blame here. Everyone is just trying to help. But do you know what this does to us? It depletes us of any sense of self-control. Suddenly our mind owns us and the only way out is to take tablets to finally "be normal."

Reclaim Your Power

Dr. Leaf is speaking out and shining a light on the lack of evidence for depression as a disease, and in turn she is giving us back our power! If depression isn't necessarily a disease, if it's potentially not a chemical imbalance, then what is it? You, too, may have thought, "Why is it happening? Why am I feeling down?"

Well, the way I see it, it is like a disease in the sense that there is a *dis-ease* in the mind and body. Depression is a clear sign that something is not right. We just need to ask that small but ever so mighty question: Why?

The power in this question is immeasurable! It's life-changing! It led me to an ADHD diagnosis. When I was left with no option but to go it alone without medication, I decided to learn all about ADHD, asking why every step of the way. I healed many of my suppressed wounds and finally made life changes that work for me. The results? Well, you're reading one of them. Let's take your power back too!

Become a Seeker of Knowledge

Now that you know it's empowering to ask why, I want you to get a little deeper into the role of investigator, especially when it comes to your mental and physical health. There are two ways to approach our health and healing: we can either be the hider or the seeker.

Medical doctors and other health-care practitioners often focus on managing symptoms by prescribing medications and giving treatments to alleviate immediate discomfort or distress. They often prioritize symptom relief without always looking for the underlying causes. You could say they hide the cause by masking the symptoms, and this works well for lots of ailments or until the root cause is found!

Functional doctors take a more holistic approach, looking to identify and address the root causes of illness. They look beyond the surface symptoms to find the underlying issues in the body, aiming to ultimately heal the core issue.

Throughout the ADHD Reset journey and perhaps in life, I want you to channel your inner functional practitioner and seek the root cause of your habits, behaviors, emotions, wounds, and so on, because we are aiming to heal and provide long-term solutions!

→ WRITE IT DOWN: Channel Your Inner Healer

To help you channel your inner functional medicine practitioner, begin to explore hiding and seeking with the following journal prompts.

This reflective practice will give you an overview of how hiding and seeking impacts your life both negatively and positively. The aim of this practice is to encourage mindfulness of how hiding can strip you of your power and to awaken your inner seeker instead.

Hiding

1. Describe a situation when you chose to hide your symptoms or feelings. How did this impact your overall well-being and sense of empowerment?
2. Recall a moment when you opened up about your hidden feelings and experienced a notable improvement in your emotional state.

Seeking

1. Explore a memory when you decided to seek answers and openly address your symptoms, concerns, or curiosity. How did this empower you?
2. List the benefits you expect to gain by adopting a mindset where you prioritize seeking answers and addressing underlying issues. How will it help you regain a sense of control?

Please acknowledge that by reading this book, you are already a seeker. You already have this mindset toward certain aspects of your life. Now you will become aware of when you hide and when you seek to truly tap into this mindset in full!

Intuitiveness and Our Inner Seeker

Often our intuitiveness triggers our inner seeker to begin exploring! As we've seen, we often become detached from our curiosity and intuition, which damages our self-esteem and trust in ourselves. From a young age, we start to hide our curiosity out of shame and fear of "being found out"

Eventually we stop trusting our gut instincts and lose confidence in our ability to understand these moments of intuitive magic. Another way that our intuition gets diluted is by mixing up this emotion with fear, stress, or anxiety.

Intuition Is Part of Your Magic Self

Intuition has been part of your magic all along, but you often don't listen to it for all these reasons. How often have you felt like kicking yourself because *you knew* something was going to happen but you didn't actually share that with anyone before whatever happened, happened? So, saying "I knew that was going to happen" makes you sound like a big, stinky liar, and instead, you keep quiet, silently bewildered by your inner knowing.

How many films have you ruined by blurting out the ending even though it's the first time you watched it? I annoyed a lot of people in the movie theater with that one when I didn't have much verbal impulse control!

How many times have you felt that gut instinct niggle in your tummy, ignored it, and then been furious with yourself for ignoring said tummy niggle? In fact, let's answer a few questions to show you just how powerful your curiosity is and how intuitively magical you are!

Grab your journal and write this down: **My Amazing Intuition**
1. Have you ever said the words "I knew it!!"?
   a. What was it about?
   b. How did you know it? Explain your feelings.
2. Reflect on a time when you had a gut feeling about something but chose not to listen to it, only to discover later that your instincts were correct.
3. Recall a time when you did listen to your intuition and how it was useful!
4. Have you ever made a friend quickly because you instantly knew you would get along with them?
5. Have you ever instinctively asked why and it resulted in some sort of discovery?

Imagine That I'm Your ADHD Reset Coach

Now that you are an intuitive seeker, we're going to do some more self-exploration. The aim of this chapter so far has been for you to trust your intuition, listen to your curious nature (see sidebar on page 27), and act on it to regain your power. I want you to feel comfortable uncovering parts of yourself that you have hidden away and to feel excited about exploring your life, body, and mind!

In real life, if you're my client, I begin a coaching consultation by learning all I can about you, your goals, and your desired outcomes. This is a crucial part of all my one-to-one coaching programs. It allows the client and coach to gain a bird's-eye view of their life.

Without guidance, this can be especially difficult when you have ADHD because our thoughts feel like a rummage sale! All the items are there but it lacks organization. This is why I body double with my ADHD clients while they self-reflect by using a form full of prompts to make it a simple task!

My form for self-exploration allows you to honestly assess what actions you are currently taking in each area of your life. This is not scoring your life but instead being mindful of the actions you currently take and, for each area, deciding if you are inactive, somewhat active, or active. Then you can decide what additional actions you would ideally take for each area to get the life results that you desire.

ADHD 101: What Is Body Doubling?

ADHD body doubling is a term coined in the late '90s by Linda Anderson, an ADHD coach with decades of experience. It's a supportive technique where you work alongside someone who acts as a "double" as you take action.

What does this mean? The double gives you a sense of accountability, assistance, and focus. This technique can support administrative work, active tasks such as cleaning, or even attending certain appointments that you may otherwise avoid without a body double!

You can also mimic having a physical body double by phoning friends to simply be with you while you get something done, providing you with someone to check in with at the start and end of tasks. You can also use planners to act as a "second brain" that guides you through your day.

I use body doubling as part of my ADHD coaching. I first started as a general life coach, and at the time, giving lots of homework was the standard thing to do. It wasn't until I had my first ADHD client that I realized this won't fly. Now I embed this kind of work within sessions and guide my clients through any written work and practices during our call. Try using this book with my words and guidance as your body double when you do the practices.

Thanks for coining the term, Linda. It makes total sense and is so helpful!

→ LIFE OVERVIEW

Before you begin, remind yourself how curiosity physically feels to you and tap into your curious nature. Relax into the practice. There is no right or wrong answer. All it requires is honesty. There is no good or bad "score." Treat this exercise like one of those fun online quizzes that tells you all about your life!

In your journal list *all the actions* you are taking in the following areas and leave space underneath your lists to write new actions later.

Health
Mind (mental health, emotional balance, and self-care):
Example of actions: "I read self-help books."
Body (physical health, fitness, and well-being):
Example: "I take my dog for daily walks."
Soul (inner peace, fulfillment, things that bring you joy):
Example: "I listen to sleep-hypnosis recordings."

Relationships
Family (dynamics, efforts, and connections):
Example: "I call my mom most days."
Romantic (intimate relationships, love life, and partnerships):
Example: "I have a movie date every week."
Friends (social connections, support networks, and friends):
Example: "I talk every day in a friendship group chat."

Career
My job/mission/dream (alignment with personal values, purpose, life goals):
Example: "I work for myself doing what I enjoy."
Money (financial well-being, stability, and abundance):
Example: "I have yearly salary increases."
Growth (professional development, learning, and personal growth):
Example: "I am reading *The ADHD Reset*."

Now, thanks to this exercise, you will have an overview for each area of your life. This is an honest look at what the current state of each area is and what actions you've taken. This will help you know where you are and ignite an intuitive feeling for where you want to be! Now go back to each area and write if you are:

> **Inactive**
> **Somewhat Inactive**
> **Active**

For any area that you feel you are somewhat inactive or completely inactive, write down actions you could take to bring this area of your life to a place that you would feel happy with. Remember, life is full of ebbs and flows. You will never have *all* areas of your life fully active. That is not only okay but completely normal!

I'm a pretty proactive person now, but because I have more actions going on in health and career, I am "somewhat inactive" in relationships! Give it a few months and I will be "active" in relationships and perhaps momentarily "inactive" in health as I splurge with friends and feed my mental health with connection!

The beauty of this perspective is that it is forever rebalancing, as long as you know what actions you can take when you feel you need to give more effort in certain areas. If you feel a little lonely, check on the actions you can take within relationships. If you feel like you have hit a brick wall in your personal development, check what actions you can take for growth! You can come back to this self-made exploration chart any time you need to remind yourself of the actions you can take.

It is not uncommon to be inactive in all areas of life. I have been there! Now that we have gone through your "coaching consultation," you'll have a better feeling of which area needs most of your attention. As we go through each chapter or each coaching session, you'll naturally lean into applying the teachings to that area of your life. You can even add new actions within each section of your life overview!

With this increased self-awareness, you can harness your strengths, adopt different behaviors, and create the desired changes. Where you are now is *exactly* where you need to be to begin your ADHD reset. Take a deep breath because we are about to get even more honest and peel off the mask you've been wearing!

→ FIVE-MINUTE RESET: Reenter the *Now*

After reflective practices, we can feel overwhelmed. Let's stretch our lungs and reset our nervous system so you feel relaxed and reenergized! Before moving on to the next chapter, let's practice the 4-7-8 breathing technique.

This practice helps you activate the parasympathetic nervous system, otherwise known as the "rest-and-digest system" because it is responsible for promoting relaxation, conserving energy, and restoring the body to a state of balance after periods of stress or activity.

Here Is How You Do It

Practice the first round as you read.

1. Take a comfortable seated position or lie down with your arms by your sides.
2. Close your eyes (once you have read the instructions, of course!) and take a few deep breaths to settle into your body.
3. Inhale quietly and deeply through your nose for a count of four seconds. Feel your lungs expand and your chest stretch as you breathe in.
4. Hold your breath for seven seconds. Focus on the energizing sensation of oxygen and how calming the stillness is within your body.
5. Exhale slowly and completely through your mouth for a count of eight seconds, emptying your lungs completely and noticing tension being released.
6. Repeat this cycle for four rounds or as many times as you feel you need to.
7. Listen to your body and stop when you feel relaxed and refreshed.

Along with activating the parasympathetic nervous system and promoting relaxation and reducing stress, this exercise brings your attention to the present moment, allowing you to let go of worries about the past or future. Additionally, the deliberate slowing of your breath can help cultivate a sense of excitement and enthusiasm for the present moment.

The Most Important Things You Need to Know

- Remember the power of asking why. Listen to your intuition, ask questions, and get answers.
- Identify how each emotion, such as intuition, makes it easier for you to understand yourself and triggers positive actions.
- Realize that listening to your intuition rebuilds your self-trust.
- As people with ADHD, our intuitive and curious nature makes us natural explorers and seekers! Activate your inner seeker by listening to your intuition.
- Remember that each area of your life will flow in and out of inactive, somewhat inactive, and active states. Viewing your life like this removes a sense of overwhelm and gives you the opportunity to feel in control.

ADHD Masking and Mirroring:

How You Have Been Coping So Far

LET'S START WITH WHERE YOU ARE NOW, which is likely using masking to cope with the world. So, what exactly does this mean? When it comes to ADHD, masking is when we camouflage our thoughts, behaviors, and emotions to hide our symptoms and pretend we're neurotypical or "normal."

Over time, this sophisticated tactic helps us adjust our actions to mimic societal norms and expectations. Think about when you sit in a movie theater and refrain from fidgeting, chatting through the film, or researching each character on your phone. This is often a response to external pressures, such as being told from a young age to be quiet; feared social judgments, such as appearing different to our peers; and the deep desire everyone feels to fit in.

Masking arises as a coping mechanism, and we often do it without thinking. It's like someone who feels anxious and automatically takes deep breaths to calm themselves.

ADHD 101:
Understanding Four Common ADHD Masking Behaviors

1. Hiding How You Feel and What You Really Think. Do You . . .
- Appear calm when feeling stressed, anxious, or overwhelmed?
- Squelch your opinions?
- Cover up your energy to appear calm?
- Suppress the urge to move, fidget, or stim?

2. Being a Perfectionist. Do You . . .
- Have extremely high standards for any work you do?
- Take on more work than you can manage?
- Check your work multiple times before submission?
- Obsessively clean and tidy?
- Become angry if something doesn't feel perfect to you?

3. Pretending to Be Like Everyone Else. Do You . . .
- Imitate the behavior of others?
- React to news in a way you think others expect you to?
- Pretend that you are not struggling with something, that you have the same interests as someone else, that you know what someone has said even if you didn't hear it?

4. Overcompensating to Appear Neurotypical. Do You . . .
- Think about not talking over someone instead of listening to them?
- Pay extra attention so you do not miss anything someone says?
- Arrive very early to events to ensure you aren't late?
- Write everything down?
- Obsessively check your belongings, to-do lists, calendar, door locks, oven knobs, keys, phone, etc.?
- Create complex organizational systems so you feel you can always find what you need?

Feeling Different Doesn't Feel Good

We often describe the ADHD experience as "feeling different," and it is this very feeling that triggers us from a young age to begin masking. If we feel different, we feel that we do not belong, and this sparks our nervous system to send signals of danger!

In our modern world, we can survive on our own, but I don't recommend it. From the beginning of time, people have evolved to live with others. In fact, many moons ago, fitting into and belonging to a group was essential for our survival!

ADHD Magic!
The Qualities You Have That Make You Special

There are many more magical parts of you, but here are a few to get you feeling sparkly!

Combined Magic & Mind Reading!
Feeling different makes us mirror those around us and become hyperaware of how others feel. Being sensitive souls, feeling our emotions deeply, and having extremely vivid imaginations means that we can put ourselves in another person's shoes with total ease. We know when someone feels down in the dumps, and we can quickly imagine how they are feeling and offer them authentic compassion. These combined qualities make us seem like mind readers!

Energy Uplifters!
Often those of us in the ADHD community are described as being goofy, silly, and funny, and that's because our brains don't do well in dull environments. If there isn't entertainment on hand, then roll up the curtains because the show is about to begin!

Our energy is so infectious that it lifts the spirits of those around us. In fact, humans mirror neurons, brain cells that fire when we perform an action and when we observe someone else performing the same action.

If we express happiness around someone who is sad, we activate mirror neurons in that person's brain, triggering a similar emotional response! It's basically a happy spell we can perform to lift anyone's mood!

Today you may use masking to fit in with your friends or to avoid feeling embarrassed when you stim, or become overstimulated, but it's rooted to our ancestral survival instincts. Because of this, removing the mask may feel difficult to do.

ADHD: Being Born with a Magic Wand

The way I like to think about ADHD and masking is that it's like being born with a magic wand with no instructions. At first the wand is of no use because we're just enjoying babbling about, being a baby. But as we grow to be a child, we use our magic wand to play the most magical make-believe!

We don't need our imagination to be fed by movies of trapped princesses in towers or knights battling to save the kingdom. We can become them, turning our bedroom into a cave of safety from the dragon, our living room cushions into stepping stones over hot boiling lava, or our garden into a wild jungle. Our mind contains scripts to never-ending adventures!

But as we get older, we start to notice that others don't seem to have the same capacity for magic as we do. We often take the lead in make-believe play because we truly see it. This usually gets mistaken for being bossy!

Still, we feel like our sparkle is unmatched by those around us, and we are very aware of this. Without adding in our sparkly magic, the world just feels . . . boring!

But pretty soon, all we really want is to just fit in, and we know that sometimes our magic makes us stand out a little too much for our liking. Our confident voice speaks up much more than others. Our constant drive to create is tiring for those who lack the energy. We have a zest for life that is way beyond our years. Put it all together and it is simply too much, or so I've been told. So, we begin to hide it.

The High Price of Fitting In

You may not express the fact that you feel things more deeply than others out of fear of being called too sensitive or being rejected. You may also stop shining as brightly as you can with your extroverted personality because you don't want to be labeled a show-off. You may also rein in your out-of-the-box creative ideas because you don't want to be seen to outshine others.

Over time, suppressing who you really are may make you forget that you have the magic wand. The person you are inside, the one with the magic, becomes totally detached from the persona you present to the world. You become ordinary. You fit in—but at a price.

Fitting in through masking feels safe, but it can also feel quite lonely because you've forged relationships by hiding who you truly are. This is a big reason why so many of us with ADHD find ourselves feeling somewhat lost and alone in life. We don't know who we are or what we really want because we've disconnected from our authentic selves!

The Fear of Being Found Out

Masking also makes us live with a fear of being "found out," which is a heavy burden to carry. Even if we aren't exactly sure who we are on the inside, we have a niggling feeling that it doesn't match who we present to others on the outside. This often causes social anxiety and stress in addition to having ADHD. We have to constantly remind ourselves to blend in, tone ourselves down, not talk too much, and mirror those around us so we know we are acting *exactly* as we should in order to belong and avoid being discovered as a "fraud."

Masking and Work

It's not just our liveliness and quirks with family, friends, and acquaintances that we must continuously conceal. We also feel the need to mask in our jobs, careers, and professions. For example, working in a corporate world forces us to appear organized, punctual, and as engaged as our colleagues seem to be in meetings. In reality, we aren't naturally great at organizing our workload, keeping track of time, or paying attention in meetings that often seem boring. The school and work systems weren't made with ADHD in mind!

When I worked in a corporate office, I would often stay later than my contractual hours. Although my job title was social media executive, the business was understaffed, so in reality I helped with everything from branding, marketing, and event planning to writing blog posts and magazine articles to doing interviews, photography, and even modeling! Like many of those with ADHD, I was overworked because of my adaptability and versatility. This meant that I often worked overtime, usually two to five hours a week.

For a short period of time there had been roadwork on my route to work, which made it very difficult to estimate the time I had to leave to get to the office by 9:00 a.m. Some days I would glide through the traffic no problem and be there by 8:30 a.m. Other days, I was late, although never more than ten minutes. Every morning I was stressed out, even though my unpaid overtime more than made up for my tardiness.

After this happened three times in one month, a manager told me that if I were late again, they would put an official write-up in my file. I tried to explain my difficulty in navigating the current roadwork and assured her that I had worked at least a week's worth of overtime. But it didn't matter.

This seemed so illogical and unfair to me. I was frustrated by her inflexibility, the rules, the corporate speak, and the fact that they didn't understand that I was actually doing a substantial amount of work for free. This boggled my ADHD brain!

From that day onward I arrived exactly on time, even if it meant I waited in my car in the morning, and I left at exactly 5:30 p.m., even if I hadn't completed the work from the many roles I was juggling. If I did have to work overtime, I let them know that I was keeping a record.

The Cost of Unmasking at Work

I had unmasked my magical ADHD traits when I worked for this company, and they bene-fited from it. They counted on me to do many creative tasks that they couldn't find others to do within their budget, but they wouldn't accept one of my undesirable ADHD traits.

At work we often mask what we deem to be undesirable, such as disorganization and time management. But when we unmask and reveal our desirable ADHD traits—multi-tasking, adaptability, creativity, and innovation—we become an easy target to exploit our skill set and time! This is why I went on a personal overtime strike during this employ-ment. We all need to stand up for ourselves.

Perfectionism and People-Pleasing

However, masking our symptoms can push us into a perfectionistic state of being. That's because we tend to overcompensate to ensure we appear "normal" or even to excel. We do this to make up for how we feel on the inside, which is often stressed, overwhelmed, insecure, and burned out from wearing our mask for lengthy periods of time. Even worse, the fear of "being found out" once again rears its head, and we fret over our inner turbulence and perceived inadequacies bubbling to the surface in front of our superiors: "They must *not* know I *ever* struggle with *any* of the work!"

A good example of perfectionism is when you recheck your sent email to make sure you attached a document. God forbid we have to send the follow-up email: "Apologies—here is the attachment. Kindest Regards, Claire!" You know that you're compensating for your busy brain and forgetfulness, but to the outside world you're an organized professional who likes to double-check all their work. No problem, right?

However, eventually perfectionism can seep into any area of your life where you feel "seen" by others. Masking makes you hyperaware of your perceived faults and can make you intolerant of flaws in others. So now you're holding not only yourself but others to your impossibly high standards, which you've adopted to hide your insecurities about your ADHD symptoms.

Another way we tend to overcompensate (especially in the workplace) is to please people. People-pleasing is exactly how I always used to end up juggling double, often triple, the workload that fell outside of my job role! It was a way for me to prove that I was more than capable.

I also wanted to be accepted, and people-pleasing is an effective way to win others' approval. After you have spent a lifetime mastering how to be accepted by your peers, people-pleasing becomes another way for you to gain this sense of acceptance in your adulthood.

Insecurity and Imposter Syndrome

ADHD masking is linked to feelings of inadequacy. As you've seen, all these masking behaviors cause a disconnect between who we present ourselves to be and how we feel about ourselves on the inside. After all, we are masking our symptoms, hiding when we struggle, pretending to be perfect, and pleasing others instead of ourselves. This is why we usually end up feeling like an imposter! Imposter syndrome is where individuals doubt their abilities and fear being exposed as frauds. This is a common recurring theme throughout a life of ADHD.

For those without ADHD, imposter syndrome is often a temporary feeling during certain periods of their life, such as starting a new job, going to university, becoming a parent, and so on. It is usually linked to when we are learning something new. However, having ADHD means we can often always feel "new" and out of our depth because we will never work in the same way as our peers.

Roles in different areas of our life can often trigger feeling like a fraud. For example, some of my coaching clients and followers have asked me why they are an organizational queen in the office but a disorganized mess at home. For all those that struggle with this, the answer isn't simply "You are masking in the office and unmasking at home." ADHD doesn't mean we are incapable of having some order in our private lives or that we are only able to have order when we fear losing our job.

Mask Burnout

What's really happening here is that we're wearing our ADHD mask too often and for far too long, so that when we get home, not only are we unmasked but completely burned out! This *combination* of unmasking *and* burnout is the reason for your untidy home, not evidence that you're a fraud at work! The more you mask, the more burned out you feel. It's a vicious circle.

Who you truly are is somewhere in the middle. You're not a perfectly clean and organized workaholic or a lazy slob. These extremes come from extreme mask-wearing burnout!

Masking: Burying Who We Truly Are

The effort required to mask symptoms places a huge emotional burden on us. If we think of masking as "burying" our true selves, it becomes clear why masking can cause us so much inner turbulence. If I say, "I often mask my stims when I feel overstimulated," this normalizes this process. But if I say, "I bury my stims when I am overstimulated," it sounds like what it is—a problem—even though it's a coping tool.

Stimming helps us self-soothe and regulate our nervous system when our mind is overstimulated. If we don't do this, and instead we bury our stims, we internalize this overstimulation. This just makes our body and brain more dysregulated, and we feel more overwhelmed. But guess what? We have a built-in, automatic de-stressing tool to use—the mask needs to come off!

ADHD 101: What Is Stimming?

ADHD stimming, also known as self-stimulatory behavior, involves the repetitive movements or sounds that individuals with ADHD often engage in unconsciously. This can include humming, pacing, fidgeting, skin picking, teeth grinding, rocking, tapping, and even hand flapping!

But why do we stim? Let's break it down—we stim to:

Enhance focus: Stimming helps us zero in on tasks.
Ride the emotion wave: It's our way of processing and managing feelings, making the world feel less overwhelming.
Beat the boredom: Stimming is our go-to activity when boredom strikes, keeping things fun and engaging.
Show some emotion: It allows us to express excitement, happiness, or any other emotion—no words needed!
Chill out: The repetitive rhythm of stimming can be calming, helping us relax and reduce stress.
Stay on task: Even with less-interesting subjects, stimming helps us stay engaged and ready to tackle them.

Stimming is our unique way of navigating the world, and it's something to embrace! Like anything else, it's all about finding what works best for each of us and owning it.

→ WRITE IT DOWN: Unmasking ADHD

Let's find out what parts of yourself you have been masking with the following journal practice.

1 **Recall instances when you consciously adapted your behavior to fit in and appear "typical." Write your examples down.** This could perhaps be a time you didn't share your bright ideas with a colleague because you've been made to feel like you shouldn't outshine others, or talking in a soft voice when naturally you have a powerful presence. Take your time and really think about how you would have behaved if you didn't have your mask on.

2 **Looking at your examples, what specific symptoms are you masking? Are you masking symptoms or personality?** Get specific about what you hide. Masking when you're sitting still watching a movie in the theater is one thing, but not joining in conversations in case you "talk too much" is refusing yourself to be . . . yourself!

3 **Reflect on the emotions and challenges faced while masking and make note of what effects they've had on your well-being.** Be mindful of instances where you masked outwardly and it may have caused internal stress, anxiety, and/or emotional dysregulation.

4 **Using your imagination, compare your behaviors masked and unmasked.** Imagine going to an event that you would enjoy—seeing your favorite musician or show perhaps. You can pick any event that you like. Then make two lists: one titled "Unmasked"; the other, "Masked." Write down your behaviors, actions, and feelings in each category and see how vastly different your experience at the event would be.

Here is an example of going to a concert:

Unmasked	Masked
• I would take noise-reducing earplugs to avoid becoming overstimulated if I need them.	• I would hide feeling anxious when it became very loud but would feel uncomfortable.
• I would sing my heart out.	• I would sing but only if others were also singing.
• I would dance when I felt like it.	• I would dance but only if others were dancing.
• I would tell my friends if I felt nervous.	• I would pay attention to what others are doing.
• I would leave whenever I wanted to.	• I would drink to settle my nerves.

Unmasking gives us freedom to be true to who we are and to live in the moment without hesitation. It gives us the chance to connect with others and seek support if we need to, instead of suffering in silence.

Masking is tiring! But sometimes it feels necessary to do. I, for one, would withstand excessively fidgeting in my seat if I were having dinner with royalty! However, I like to think that I have finally put down the personality part of the mask, such as authentically adding my opinion into conversation. I try to be adaptable depending on the situation I'm in.

Masking, Mirroring, and Adaptability

Being adaptable and wearing a mask are often mixed up. An old friend of mine once pointed out that I seem to "change" depending on who I am with. I exclaimed, "I'm a chameleon!" and "I bounce off other people's energy!" which didn't seem to ease their concern much at all.

The conversation stuck with me. *I had been found out!!* It made me reflect on my personality and my mask wearing in my undiagnosed ADHD days. I was confused by the conversation.

Who am I? I had to really figure out when I was being myself, when I was pretending to be someone else without realizing it, and when I was appropriately adapting to the environment I was in. I looked at exactly what it means to be adaptable. It means to have the ability to adjust or change easily in response to different circumstances, situations, or environments. It is not "changing who you are to be socially accepted."

ADHD: Keeping It Simple

The Difference between Masking, Mirroring, and Adaptability

Masking
ADHD masking is when individuals hide or compensate for their ADHD symptoms, often concealing their true challenges, symptoms, and abilities.

Mirroring
ADHD mirroring is when individuals mimic the behaviors or interests of others to fit in socially.

Adaptability
ADHD adaptability is a skill individuals use to effectively navigate situations and tasks, leveraging their dynamic, creative, and flexible thinking, as well as their problem-solving skills.

You can be described as adaptable if you are able to juggle several job roles and skills, handle an emergency, or help someone in need. It can also mean being able to be professional during a work meeting and casual and relaxed in the office. You aren't pretending to be something; you have just adapted to the circumstances.

Masking and Mirroring

Mirroring is another aspect of ADHD masking. Masking means hiding parts of yourself to fit in. Mirroring is when you watch someone else and act the way they do. Just like masking, mirroring—or wearing someone else's mask—isn't a conscious choice. It is another reflex to try to navigate the world with hidden ADHD.

Adopting others' behavior can be an effective way to gain social acceptance. After years of masking our magic and trying to fit in, it makes sense that we mirror others to have smoother interactions that help us avoid rejection. If we are like them, how can they not accept us? It also shows just how unbelievably adaptive we are! Mirroring can be a useful skill to use when we want to fit in at work or social situations. Try to use it as needed and not make it a way of life. Ultimately, it's important to be true to yourself, not a copy of others.

It is no wonder so many actors have ADHD. They have lived their lives being different characters just to cope—they may as well get paid for it!

- Johnny Depp is a late-diagnosed actor who has played a wide range of complex characters. Perhaps the ADHD versatility played a part in this!
- Mark Ruffalo, most famous for playing the Hulk, said in a video with Child Mind Institute about growing up with ADHD: "One of the things that was very difficult for me was grade school—feeling very strange and unique and freakish, feeling like I didn't fit in anywhere." I bet the masks he wore to fit in throughout life got him that bit closer to wearing the Hulk mask!
- Paris Hilton, who has ADHD and convinced the world she had a childlike voice and only cared for all things pink, has since appeared on ITV's *This Morning* and explained in her natural deeper voice, "This is my real voice; that was just a character I was playing." She admittedly played for an entirely different character than who she truly is for decades! It's like she said, "I have ADHD, and I'll make it work for me!"

Masking versus Adaptability

You can see that masking is a coping mechanism. It's a skill we learn to avoid judgment, conceal our symptoms, and minimize attention to what we think are our undesirable ADHD traits.

Adaptability, including mirroring, however, is rooted in ADHD's cognitive strengths. It involves quick thinking, problem-solving, and embracing change. Unlike masking, this type of adaptation isn't about hiding who you are but rather using strengths and show-ing your versatility to gain a sense of control and guaranteed acceptance.

For example, as a child, I had elocution lessons. Now, if I were to meet someone im-portant—like, say, royalty—I'd be sure to speak with proper pronunciation. But this isn't masking. This would be me using a skill I have in an environment that it's suited to. That, my friend, is the magical ADHD skill of adaptability.

Unmasking and Finding Your Magic

With this in mind, look over your answers to the Unmasking ADHD journal practice and circle anything you may have written down that demonstrates adaptability. Then put a star next to it to symbolize the magic you have just rediscovered! Masking has a bad rep, and therefore it may live in your unconscious as a "negative trait" of being ADHD. By revealing when you have been adaptable as opposed to masking, you will reframe this ability into pure ADHD magic. This is a strength you have!

If none of your current answers are examples of adaptability, think of moments where you have been able to adapt to a situation and when you have mirrored others. Then write them down. This will help you identify the difference between when you mask, when you mirror, and when you adapt.

When you realize how much you have masked and what its purpose is, you may feel like you can't survive without it. You can.

Stick with me and you'll learn how to switch from ADHD masking to managing ADHD! It starts with acknowledging and accepting your neurodivergent identity, feeling comfortable to be your magical self, letting the mask go, and leaning into your adaptability as and when you want to. Once the fact that you have ADHD is no longer a secret and you no longer feel the need to hide who you are, you'll be able to openly manage your ADHD without a mask.

As unique and magical as we are, masking is actually something that everyone does to some degree, ADHD or not! Everyone hides parts of themselves they deem undesirable, and we sometimes get it wrong and hide the most amazing things about ourselves. This part of a person is called shadow self, and we are going to shine a light on your shadows next!

→ BE PRESENT RESET

You have been reflecting on your life an awful lot during this chapter. You have done some great work, but we don't want to leave your mindset stuck in the past!

To bring you back to the now, name in your mind:

- Five things you can see that are green, white, or blue
- Four things you can touch in your environment and make note of how they feel
- Three things you can hear (even if it is your own breath or movement, if you're in a quiet space)
- Two things you can smell (even if you have to actively smell something like your own sleeve or the pages of this book)
- One thing you can taste

Now take three nice long deep inhales and exhales at your own comfortable pace.

Finally, in your mind or out loud, say, "I am here, right now in this very moment."

Great job! Welcome back to the now.

The Most Important Things You Need to Know

- Unmask your built-in coping skills! Masking is a form of coping, but sometimes we accidentally mask even better coping skills that we have, such as stimming to regulate our nervous system, deep breathing to calm ourselves down, talking through our feelings, and so on.
- Mirroring is copying someone else's behavior, masking is hiding parts of yourself, and adaptability is using your different skills for different environments or scenarios.
- Unmasking gives you the freedom to be true to who you are!
- Unmasking helps to avoid burnout! Wearing your mask for too long can result in feeling exhausted.

How Shadow Work Can Help You:

Unmask Yourself and Reveal Your Magic

THE CONCEPT OF "SHADOW SELF" refers to the parts of yourself that you unconsciously suppress, deny, or reject. This is different from masking, as we often knowingly mask parts of ourselves but our shadow self can be hidden unconsciously. For example, you may feel ashamed that you need your parents' support as an adult, so you deny this part of yourself and reject the offer of a place to stay. Or you strive to make a lot of money to seek total freedom and comfort, but you hide this part of yourself for fear of being judged negatively by those who deem money to be "the source of all evil." Everyone's shadows are not necessarily the same.

Discovering your shadow self can be a little uncomfortable because you are revealing the undesirable parts of who you are. The best way to travel through this part of your ADHD Reset journey is to maintain your curiosity throughout and reflect on your shadow self with total honesty. You'll soon realize that some qualities that you have pushed into the depths of your shadow self are in fact bright and beautiful parts of your personality.

A common shadow for men is to conceal their kind and sensitive traits to protect their masculine persona. Basically they file them away into the negative filing cabinet within the brain instead of the positive one.

Why Shadow Work Is So Important

The aim of shadow work is to cast a light on the parts of yourself that you have kept in the dark. To live with full authenticity and self-awareness, you have to do this work. Specifically for the ADHD community, because we have become such experts at masking, shadow work helps us reveal parts of ourselves we may have accidentally hidden away—more so than those without ADHD. Once you have discovered your shadows, I'll guide you through gently integrating your shadows back into who you authentically are with full acceptance.

Integrating shadows does not mean you will "become them," as they already live within you. We avoid uncomfortable parts of ourselves, but that doesn't mean they do not exist. They are there, waiting backstage in your unconscious mind, but you simply deny them any show time. Integration simply means that you are no longer hiding these parts from yourself and are becoming consciously aware of these authentic aspects of yourself with self-acceptance and love.

Until you make the unconscious conscious, it will direct your life and you will call it fate.
—Carl Jung

The History of Shadow Work

The psychoanalyst Carl Jung coined the term *shadow* during his research into the psyche in 1910. Now it is used far and wide within the world of mental well-being, but I'm always surprised by how many are still unaware of this liberating and powerful self-acceptance work. Carl Jung was definitely ahead of his time!

The Persona, the Self, and the Shadow

Here is a slightly simplified model of the psyche that Jung originally made:

In the model of the psyche, you can see the "persona." Imagine this being at the front of your head. The persona is what we show to the outer world. It can also be seen as the mask we wear to hide our perceived flaws.

Outer world

PERSONA
EGO
SELF
SHADOW
ANIMA/ANIMUS

Inner world

It's important to note that this model was created for every single person, not just those with ADHD. However, now that you know wearing a mask has become an important part of concealing being neurodivergent, it's evident why shadow work is even more crucial for someone who has ADHD. We have masked our entire being, so there are plenty of shadows to shed light on and lovingly accept.

As you can see, there are several elements to Jung's psyche model, but we are going to focus on just three of those elements. The *persona* is a part of our conscious mind, the *self* lives in both the conscious and unconscious, and the *shadow* is hidden at the back of our mind like a pair of forgotten beloved jeans in the depths of our closet. Just like those jeans, our shadow is not all negative!

Jung considered everything that lives in our unconscious mind as a shadow, because it is the hidden, unknown part of ourselves. It's made up of hidden desires, unmet needs, behaviors, or characteristics that bring us a sense of shame.

However, we also have unfulfilled potential living in our unconscious and the ability to learn new skills that we never consciously thought possible!

All Shadows Are Not Negative

When I first learned that not all shadows are negative, I wondered how they could possibly become a shadow to begin with. But just like masking the magical parts of ADHD to seek acceptance, we do this with our entire personality from childhood. We unconsciously learn what is "right" and "wrong," what is desirable and undesirable. Just as we judge other people's actions on an unconscious level, we do the same with ourselves. Everything gets filtered through an internal judgment system and is either deemed acceptable and safe to display or plunged into the depths of our shadow self.

ADHD Magic! The Benefits of Your Persona

Here are benefits to masking and having a persona.

- Masking can be a solid coping mechanism that keeps us from sinking into low moods. Take laughter therapy: You fake laugh, but your body responds like it's real! Masking with a smile can sometimes result in us genuinely feeling happier!
- The persona can help us feel in control when we are in an environment of authority. Before I step into important meetings or appointments, despite feeling vulnerable, I tap into having a confident, badass persona. Suddenly I *am* confident!

It's all about having self-awareness and acceptance of your shadow and then finding balance. You have the ability to pick and choose when to lead with your persona or when to be unapologetically yourself.

Over time, we learn exactly what actions get us love, positive attention, and acceptance, and what does not! In a child's mind, this is a life-and-death situation. The way we are wired means that love and acceptance equals our survival. Without this, it's game over. This is why Jung's work is applicable to everyone. We all alter, mask, shift, and hide parts of ourselves to avoid rejection—namely, death!

Shadows and Survival

As we figure out what works and what does not to "keep us alive," we begin to hide more and more of ourselves until those parts that make us who we are become shadows. What is left is the persona.

As we go through life, we face more difficulties, heartbreak, and rejection. Each time we feel rejected, we analyze why, make adjustments, and move ahead with a little less of our authentic self at the surface. The primal dread of being deserted by our community, intricately tied to our survival instincts, far outweighs our yearning for authenticity. This is precisely why delving into shadow work often stirs up a sense of fear within us. But believe me, it is so worth it.

Limiting Beliefs and Shadow Work

If you have ADHD, you're often told that you either lack something or you are "too much" of something else. This can form limiting beliefs that are *not* shadows. We'll delve into and target your limiting beliefs in chapter 5, but for the purpose of doing this shadow work, they often show up as negative "I am" statements, such as "I am stupid" or "I am lazy." Both of these statements are examples of my old limiting beliefs, and both are completely untrue. Limiting beliefs are exactly that . . . beliefs, not fact!

However, "shadows" are *truthful* parts of our authentic self that we have shunned away because we have unconsciously deemed them to be undesirable and believe they put us at risk of being disliked or worse, abandoned.

Often when we begin shadow work, we lead with conscious thinking and let our limiting belief–based thoughts direct the shadow work by accident. So, to reiterate, limiting beliefs are untruthful beliefs that bubble up and make us think of many negative "I am" statements that we don't necessarily hide from others. In fact, we often shout about them and exclaim them openly: "I am so stupid!" "I am not good enough to do that!" Our shadows, however, are hidden truths about ourselves that we do not share with anyone. These may include hidden desires to succeed; hidden needs, such as therapy; hidden behaviors, such as stimming; and traits we suppress, such as being loud. These hidden truths can bring you a sense of shame.

ADHD: Keeping It Simple

The Consequences of Not Facing Our Shadow Selves

Shadows live within us and can manifest and spill out unexpectedly in undesirable and unhealthy ways. Suppressing our true desires or needs means they all go unmet or unfulfilled. They can show up as jealousy because our hidden desires haven't been met, or resentment and bitterness because we haven't met our needs; or they can manifest as depression, anxiety, codependency, self-sabotage, procrastination, anger, frustration, discontentment, and apathy, to name a few. Although our shadows are hidden in our subconscious, they still have a powerful impact on our outer world and overall life. So not very hidden at all when you think about it!

Living without the authenticity of shedding a light on your shadows results in your life becoming misaligned from what you are really here to do. This is why so many people struggle to answer "What is your life's purpose?" We're trying to find the answer solely based on our persona and not based on our full authentic self, which includes our shadows—that is, our hidden needs, desires, and qualities!

Until you uncover your shadows, show yourself love and grace and self-acceptance, and let go of parts of your persona that have been keeping your true self hidden, your shadows will continue to play havoc, like caged animals desperately seeking freedom to simply be.

My Shadow Self

When I began my career and started looking for jobs, I often gravitated toward those that paid well. But a few unfortunate life events convinced me that money was bad. So, the fact that I was ashamed of wanting to be financially successful became my shadow.

Shadows are really your wounded self that has adapted to avoid being hurt again. After my hurt, I associated the desire to have money with greed, unkindness, and disloyalty, and I buried my own desire for money. I unconsciously cast this shadow so far out of reach that I forged a new path and found myself working for a charity on average pay while volunteering for a nonprofit I cofounded outside of the nine-to-five.

I refused any paid posts on social media regardless of my growing following because it felt disingenuous. I only accepted freebies for sharing other people's businesses and products to be kind. I would not do it for money. I was determined to keep my desire for money a secret not only from the outside world but also from myself!

Working in the charitable sphere, I also surrounded myself with very charitable people. That wasn't a bad thing; however, many from these communities had strong opinions of "the man"—those who "take, take, take" and don't do things selflessly. This tightened the lock on the shadow I had already formed after being taken advantage of financially in the past. I had a new view of money being a tool to help others but never myself. It makes sense that I formed a shadow of shame about desiring to be financially free. My persona was the opposite of the shadow. After I did some shadow work, I realized, "Hey, you know what? I like money. It's sort of helpful to have it, and I'd like some more so I can live in the exact way I desire!"

Today, I have progressed from living with my parents and having little to nothing to having my own home with stunning countryside views. I take a couple of holidays in the sun every year. I work for myself, proudly making money from social media and my *for-profit* (because I deserve it) coaching business! This is how life-changing shadow work can be. I truly believe that without shadow work I wouldn't be where I am today.

ADHD 101: Common Shadows

Here are ten examples of common shadows—typically undesirable traits that have been suppressed and hidden—I have found amongst the ADHD community:

- Being too lively, energetic, and loud
- Needing support as an adult at home and in the workplace
- Finding spaces that are loud and busy overstimulating and stressful
- Desiring luxury items and wanting to spend money on ourselves often
- Not enjoying working for others
- Having the desire to create things
- Being sensitive
- Being inconsistent with moods and energy levels
- Having big, out-of-the-box ideas and opinions
- Having unhealthy coping methods, such as smoking, drinking alcohol, and binge eating

Does this desire make me greedy, unkind, or disloyal, as I once thought? Not at all. In fact, since letting myself live with this authenticity and gaining an understanding of why I shunned this part of myself after being hurt, I have helped more people than would have ever been possible when I was a flat-out broke do-gooder!

But I hear you—desiring money as a shadow isn't necessarily ADHD specific. Although the fear of not having control of my spending (as many with ADHD struggle with), if I did have money, definitely played a part in this shadow too!

→ WRITE IT DOWN: Cast Light on Your Shadow

Write a list of your shadows by asking yourself, "What parts of myself do I hide or keep secret from others? What parts of myself do I feel embarrassed or ashamed of?" Example: Stimming in public, desiring to open your own shop, being sensitive, desiring more friends.

Take your time and really reflect on what parts of yourself you would not like others to know about and feel that you have been shamed into hiding. Remember, these also include your desires, wants, and needs, not just undesirable behaviors, traits, and symptoms.

Once you have your shadow list, you are going to accept these parts of yourself by using the "best-friend perspective" method and a reframing technique.

Use the best-friend perspective. For each shadow listed, visualize a loved one opening up and telling you this about themselves and you offering them love, compassion, and support—with kindness, not judgment.

We are often much kinder to our loved ones than we are to ourselves. This method will help you tap into the love and compassion you hold within. Visualizing this will project the love and care onto someone else, then you can reflect it back to yourself.

For example, I would tell my "best friend" that they deserve money for all the hard work they do. Money is linked to our survival in this modern world and everyone deserves to be financially comfortable.

I would reassure her that her desire is not selfish and that she will be able to fulfil her dreams and help more people if she doesn't have to worry about money.

Write down what you would say to a best friend if they told you they try to hide this part of themselves or feel embarrassed and ashamed. Writing is a powerful way to imprint a new way of thinking into your mind. It may help to imagine you are writing a text message in response to your friend, but use your name and read the message to yourself once it's written.

Here is an example for the shadow "Being too lively, energetic, and loud":

> Aw, [*your name*], that really sucks that you feel like you are too much for people and have to tone yourself down! I love that you have a strong presence, and I'd like to see more of it!

> When you let go and laugh, you light up the *entire* room, and everyone around you can't help but join in. You literally make everyone you talk to smile, and that's so beautiful!

> I love seeing you talk passionately about the things you love too. But I completely get that sometimes you feel conscious of what other people think and try to tone it down—it's okay to feel like this. Love you.

Reframe each shadow. The reframing technique shifts our perspective, taking something from being perceived as solely negative to neutral or even positive! This will help you integrate the shadow and accept it as being a part of your authentic self. It will reduce shame and fear of judgment.

To do this, add positive benefits of you having the shadow, if you can. This is sometimes difficult but very rarely impossible! I have reframed all the shadows I have uncovered within myself and even used the reframing technique for some traumatic experiences I needed to heal from in order to move forward.

Give your subconscious mind *as much evidence as you can* for the shadow being an acceptable part of yourself that is still worthy of love. Get into a role-play mindset of having to present this evidence in the court of law! Add as much as you can and make it impossible to argue against. The more evidence you give, the easier the shadow will be released from being suppressed and in control.

An example of how to begin this reframing technique is on the next page. I have used "energetic and lively" as the example of a shadow, as we often push this part of ourselves into our shadow self due to criticism from others.

Being [*insert shadow. Example: energetic and lively*] has meant . . .

Then add all the positive benefits you can come up with! Finally finish it with:

I am so glad that I am [*insert shadow. Example: energetic and lively*].

Here is the full example of how to reframe your shadows:

Being energetic, lively, and loud has meant I have always found it really easy to make friends. As a child, I had a pleasant disregard of other people's social anxieties because I was naturally outwardly confident and didn't relate, so I would make friends with the "quiet ones" if I felt they were being left out. I really noticed when others were much quieter than I was.

It's also helped me present things well in school and the workplace and make people feel comfortable in my presence when doing so. I seem to put people at ease very quickly because I fill up any void with chatter, lighthearted laughter, and fun energy.

Having this go-go-go energy has always meant that I try new things and seek out fun things to do, and I have achieved an awful lot for my age! I have bags of experience because of this and friends from all over the place! If I wasn't energetic, lively, and loud, I don't think I would have dared to do lots of things I have done, such as show up on social media, host a festival, give public talks, walk up to and speak to the cute guy at an event who is now my husband!!! *I am so glad that I am energetic, lively, and loud!*

The goal is to find the "hidden happiness." Like when you hear someone's challenging success story: "If *that* didn't happen, I would never be where I am today!"

Some shadows are easier to reframe than others. In those cases, try shifting to a best-friend perspective, if that helps you. If you are having difficulty with reframing a part of your shadow self, be patient because this is a challenging practice. Continue coming back to seeking the hidden happiness—the collateral beauty!

For example, being very sensitive likely means you understand people's hardships better than most and have a lot of compassion. Needing support as an adult in your home and workplace may mean that you have found ways to support yourself and become an expert in a specific area of mental health.

Perhaps it has meant you have developed ways to be able to ask for help from others without much of an ego. You may enjoy helping others because you know what it feels like to need help yourself! This could have led you down certain career paths, making connections with certain loved ones . . . There are always hidden graces that are born from life's challenges. You just need to want to find the masked magic!

Accept Each Shadow with Love

You can go through this process of accepting for every shadow you have. Accept each of them one by one with love and kindness using the best-friend perspective and then change how it feels to you using the reframing technique.

The reframing technique is emotionally challenging, and it's not unusual for it to trigger a sense of conflict. Afterall, you are dismantling the story you have been telling yourself—that you have needed to wear your mask tightly and keep yourself hidden for your own survival!

The ADHD Reset is all about realistically and lovingly turning a negative into a positive. Next, you'll learn how to rewrite your story and switch to a positive growth mindset.

The Most Important Things You Need to Know

- Shadow self refers to the parts of yourself that you unconsciously suppress, deny, or reject.
- When discovering your shadows, maintain your curiosity throughout and reflect on your shadow self with total honesty. This will also help you transition into your growth mindset.
- If we don't lovingly accept our shadow self, our unmet true desires can spill out in unhealthy and undesirable ways, such as jealousy, resentment, bitterness, and self-hate.
- Using the best-friend perspective lets us tap into the self-love we have within us that we have often rejected from being overly critical and having damaged our self-love, confidence, and worth.

Rewrite Your Story:
See the Glass as Half Full, Not Half Empty

DID YOU KNOW THAT YOUR THOUGHTS are the result of how you have trained your brain? Our mind remembers the same way the body does when we learn a new dance step. Most thoughts are not brand-new. They are recycled. This is why changing the way you think can feel difficult, because all your thoughts are habitual.

I used to wake up and if I saw rain, I would moan and groan about the weather— "Another dull day!" Through years of accidentally training myself to think this way, my negative perception of rain was automatic. Ironically, I didn't think about my thoughts. I instantly reacted and perceived the rain as a negative start to my day. It wasn't until I started challenging my thinking and perceptions that I realized just how damaging a little thought like this can be!

Thoughts → Emotions → Actions

Our thoughts trigger our emotions, and our emotions have a direct impact on the actions we choose to take. I refer to this natural cycle throughout your ADHD reset because it is *that* important to understand in full.

With my morning rainy-day thoughts, I would trigger negative emotions, and the actions that I took on that morning would alter and reflect my glass-half-empty attitude. I would stay in bed longer, scroll on my phone instead of being present, leave my curtains closed, skip the morning walk or run, all because my perception of the day was negative due to . . . the rain! Living in drizzly England, you can guess how this could become quite problematic for me.

I wanted to change this, so I began to learn more about how our conscious thoughts and our subconscious beliefs influence how we feel.

How You (and Others) Think about ADHD

Our perception of life controls our entire being. If something as insignificant as rain can affect our mood, think about what our perception of more serious things can cause us to do and be. Let's start with the perception of ADHD.

Commonly, ADHD is perceived by those without it as someone who is hyper, struggles to focus, and perhaps loud! You know it's so much more than this! But this very common perception is problematic because it causes so much misunderstanding, a lack of support, and deep frustrations.

Years ago, ADHD was even thought to be something that affects male children only. It was considered a disorder in children and often perceived as something those children would grow out of. Today, many still think you have to be extremely, outwardly hyperactive to have ADHD. The subtler combined and inattentive ADHD types were not even on the map! This lack of understanding has caused lots of issues when it comes to the public's perception of ADHD.

People may think that ADHD is:

- Serious
- Not serious at all
- Embarrassing to have
- Trendy and cool to have
- Not even real
- Very real!
- A mental health issue
- A physical difference in our brains and bodies

ADHD 101: What Is It?

Let's take a closer look at what ADHD really is. ADHD is a neurodevelopmental disorder that affects children *and* adults. Various studies (such as found in the *Expert Review of Neurotherapeutics*) using functional magnetic resonance imaging (fMRI) and structural MRI have shown that individuals with ADHD often have differences in certain brain regions compared to those without the disorder. These differences involve areas responsible for attention, impulse control, and executive functioning.

ADHD is not:
- Something that makes you less intelligent
- A character flaw or personality trait
- A result of bad parenting
- Something that can be outgrown
- Something thousands of doctors are lying about because Joe Troll Bloggs on Instagram thinks he knows better than them
- Something that millions of people are lying about having
- Caused by a lack of discipline
- Something that only affects children
- Hyperactivity
- Being lazy
- Only managed through medication

What do you agree or disagree with? Your perception of ADHD is unique, based on your life story, your belief system, and the people and things that have influenced you. Do you view ADHD negatively or positively, or perhaps both?

Regardless of exactly what ADHD is, it can mean different things to different people. This can be frustrating to the ADHD community who have a full and broader understanding of what it is in all of its permutations. Whatever your thoughts are on ADHD, you likely have been influenced by other people's negative and limited perceptions and have had a glass-half-empty mindset around having ADHD at some point.

The Power of Perception

You can't control what others think, but understanding the truth about ADHD can help you feel better about yourself. Yes, ADHD comes with its challenges, but with the right tools and mindset, none are unmanageable. ADHD also means you have a long list of incredible abilities, such as your sensitive nature that makes you incredibly caring of others and your fast-paced thoughts that can feel like a lot but give you so many amazing ideas. Even your dopamine-chasing tendencies, if managed, can be transformed into an extremely desirable trait of making boring situations fun and going after your dreams! This is exactly where we need to focus to shift your perspective.

Mental versus Physical Health

We filter all information that is presented to us—every situation, every conversation, every single word. As some of the words we hear go through an unconscious filtering system, we apply our existing experiences and conditioning to them.

Consider the term *mental health*. What comes to mind? Does it evoke positive or negative feelings? What thoughts or images arise?

Now think about the term *physical health*. Does this term feel negative or positive? What emotions or images do you associate with it?

When asked about mental health, people often have negative associations, such as stress, anxiety, or depression. It can trigger images of someone feeling sad or lonely, making us feel heavy just by thinking about it.

In contrast, thoughts about physical health vary. If you've struggled with physical health, it might trigger negative feelings. If you're healthy, it can be a neutral or even positive term, bringing feelings of gratitude and uplifting images.

If I post on social media "Journaling for my mental health today," it might imply there's something negative happening in my life or that I'm feeling emotionally troubled. However, saying "Going on a run for my physical health today" usually suggests that I'm in good shape, not that I have poor physical health.

Seeing Things Clearly

I want you to strip back your perceptions and look at the implications they may have on your thoughts and life. If we accept every negative perception that we have as being true, we risk losing ourselves—just as I did many times every day I woke up to rain. I had to challenge my perception and think about where it came from.

Movies often show scenes of sadness in the rain and scenes of happiness in the sun. My childhood taught me that when it rains, I play less, stay indoors, and feel bored. None of this has to be my perception now! I have had moments of total joy being caught in the rain.

The Victim Mindset

In chapter 1 we briefly looked at what the victim mindset is. But now it's time to ask yourself if you have a victim mindset and, if so, if you're ready to change to a growth mindset?

If you have a victim mindset, you perceive things to be happening *to* you. You may refuse responsibility, blame others, or feel disempowered to take control of your life. You may feel that no matter what you do, it won't work out for you—that you cannot change your circumstances or your future. You may tend to have an "I can't" attitude, complete with multiple reasons to prove exactly why you can't.

Often a victim mindset is developed through traumatic experiences, hardships, and setbacks. Feeling a lack of control during these times, individuals may cope by rejecting any sense of control for new difficult situations, proclaiming, "I can't control it anyway, so why bother?" You start to see yourself as a victim of each new challenge life presents.

A negative view of life forms when you feel no control over what happens. In a paradoxical way, accepting this lack of control becomes a means of feeling in control. Ironically, this perceived lack of control now feels safe because it means you can stay exactly where you are. You can say "I can't" even if you can. You can ignore the difficult-to-do self-reflection and blame others for things going wrong, arguments you have, challenging situations, and failings.

Thinking about how you identify with your ADHD label, do you see yourself in this description of the victim mindset at all? Have you let go of your sense of self control?

Negative Thoughts and the Victim Mindset

Studies suggest we have thousands of thoughts per day! Surprisingly, most of these thoughts are negative. If we aren't mindful of the quality of our thoughts, we can slip into the victim mindset and other depressive states that can eventually rule our life.

On the contrary, positive thinking can also rule our world! With every positive thought we have, we trigger positive emotions and therefore are more likely to act in more positive and beneficial ways.

We need to focus on being habitually positive thinkers, and that is exactly what I am about to show you how to do!

ADHD: Keeping It Simple

Why a Victim Mindset Isn't Good for Our ADHD Community

Our brains thrive on stimulation—both positive and negative. We like the extremes of hormones, it seems. Lots and lots of dopamine or a surge of spiky cortisol. This will be explored in full when we take a closer look at our emotions later in your ADHD reset. However, I need to mention it now because it is vital that you see the connection between having ADHD and how you can easily slip into the victim mindset—just like I did.

I can guarantee we ADHDers have all experienced challenging lives, which is exactly why I widened my life coaching to include ADHD coaching. I knew my community needed more tailored support. What I have noticed through doing this work is that people often don't want the solutions. I know this is not you because you are here!

I receive thousands of comments on my social accounts, and I can easily see who genuinely wants support and who has unknowingly slipped into the victim mindset, refusing any of the support I offer. I even see people arguing within my comment threads about their ADHD symptoms, almost like they're having a "who is more ADHD" battle!

This sort of competitive victimhood is worrying because the amount of energy they use to cement their victim mindset could be used to adopt a liberating growth mindset! And this is exactly what you are going to do.

ADHD Magic! Super Thinkers

People with ADHD experience a higher frequency of thoughts or a more rapid flow of ideas compared to those without ADHD. This is commonly known as "hyper thinking" or "racing thoughts." I prefer the term *super thinkers*, to strip away the negative association and perceive it for the positive that it is!

Our minds are constantly active with many thoughts being "thunk" fast! The overactivity can contribute to an increased quantity of thoughts—that is, we think more than others!

Here's the good news. If we think more than others, and those thoughts are lightning fast, then we can very quickly create new neural pathways with a flood of positive thoughts!

It's commonly reported by the ADHD community that we have a very strong inner monologue, being able to speak in our mind and hear our own thoughts with crystal clear clarity, as if spoken out loud. This makes it even easier for us to be able to take notice of what our thoughts are and to direct our thoughts if we try to. The combination of having a strong inner voice, a high sense of self-awareness, and the ability to think fast makes us total super thinkers!

How Our Thoughts Become Habitual

Our thoughts become habitual in the following ways:

1. **Neural pathways:** Our thoughts are created through interactions among brain cells via electrical signals.
2. **Strengthening pathways:** Repeated thoughts or behaviors strengthen the connections between neurons, like forming a clear path by walking the same route often.
3. **Automatic thoughts:** As pathways strengthen, thoughts or behaviors become automatic, like driving a familiar route without thinking about it.
4. **Feedback loop:** Repeated thought patterns reinforce themselves through cues, routines, and rewards. For example, self-pity can lead to comfort eating, which provides a dopamine reward, reinforcing both the self-pity and eating habit.
5. **Energy conservation:** Habitual thoughts save mental energy, requiring less cognitive effort to execute and freeing up brain resources for other tasks.

The wonderful thing about the mind is that we can create new neural pathways whenever we want, and we can make our current neural pathways redundant. Just like if we stopped walking down a clear trodden pathway through the woods, it would eventually be absorbed by Mother Nature once again.

→ MINDSET RESET: Practice Being Kind to Your Inner Child

In order for you to feel a true desire to stop thinking negatively, you need to see yourself as the vulnerable and innocent version of you that you need to protect. You can do this by connecting to your inner child. Looking at an old photograph of yourself when you were little really helps make a quick connection, or you can visualize your younger self.

Next, write down a few of the negative things you often say to yourself that you would never let a child hear. (Brutally honest) example: "I f*cking hate my life!"

Now, take a moment to imagine that you as a young child heard you say this and understandably became upset, so you need to comfort and apologize to them.

This is what you are going to do every time you say something unkind or negative about yourself or your life. You will:

1. Recognize the thought.
2. Halt the thought process.
3. Say "I'm sorry" and something kind, preferably "I love you."

As I do this, it helps to place my hand on my chest and pretend that I am talking to my inner child, the most vulnerable version of myself who is easily upset by unkindness. I give myself a moment and say in my own mind, "I'm sorry for saying that. I didn't mean it. I love you." Then I carry on with my day knowing that I have protected myself from my own negative thoughts.

The first day I did this, I lost count of how many times I had to say sorry to myself—it was easily over fifty times—but I realized that I was also saying "I love you" over fifty times too! I was showing true loving self-compassion repeatedly throughout the day, when just the day before I was repeatedly saying awful things without any regard to the damage I was doing. This little practice alone is life-changing.

Remove Negative Influences and Feel Better

Another way to disrupt the negativity is to disrupt downers, whether it's people, places, or things.

To begin, give your media consumption an overhaul, from the TV programs you watch to the social accounts you follow. For me, my biggest negative-thinking triggers were the news and social media accounts focused on how someone looks. I put myself on a total news ban. I never missed out on anything important; news has a way of seeping into your life, especially now that we live in such a digital world. I just made sure I reduced it and didn't proactively seek it out.

Next, I removed many people from my following list and began to follow people who gave me positive thoughts. I even follow happy news accounts that are often filled with the cutest animal stories as well as some wholesome humans-being-kind kind of stories!

As a result, my feed now feeds *me* positive thoughts, empowerment, and knowledge instead of triggering negative comparisons, sucking me into the latest cancel culture, and leaving me feeling like the world is an awful place!

As for the people you surround yourself with, this takes a little longer than spending five minutes following and unfollowing! This comes with time. As you step deeper into your growth mindset and start feeling more positive, those that cause you to feel negative will seem like they have a bright flashing cone on their head with waving red flags! Toxic relationships will seep to the surface and you will easily be able to filter them out.

Cultivate Gratitude

Cultivating gratitude is a wonderful way to challenge negative thoughts and change your perspective. This proven wellness technique is one of the easiest ways to lift your mood, increase your overall well-being, and trigger happier emotions.

When you first begin your gratitude practice, it may feel a little forced. Being thankful for things we usually never give much thought to is bound to feel unfamiliar.

Start with something that you think of as negative but reframe it in a positive way. For example, when it comes to drizzly weather, I asked myself, "What is positive about rain?" Actually, I adore greenery—the lush fields and thick forests that need to be watered. My dog loves the rain; it sends her all silly, doing zoomies as the muddy puddles splat in her face! It gives so many little animals a drink. It's really not a reason for me to slump in bed and taint the day. I'm grateful for the rain.

It's also good to practice gratitude at the end of the day. So before you go to bed at night, simply select "your best bits." Replay your day and highlight the moments that made you smile or that you want to show thanks for. I have found that even on some of my gloomiest days, I can find hidden little gems.

If I ever struggle to identify things that have happened to me that day that I am grateful for, then I simplify the practice further and go over everything I have in my life that I am grateful for. This can include my eyesight, the ability to read and write, my working legs, even the bed that I am lying in as I think the thoughts!

Searching for "your best bits" is challenging your perception, reframing situations, and practicing gratitude all rolled into one. We need to do this with having ADHD too. If we don't, we slip into a victim mindset.

→ WRITE IT DOWN: Gratitude Practice

If you want to lean into gratitude on a deeper level, either as a daily wellness habit or a mood lifter when you need it, writing it down works best.

Write down what you are grateful for with lots of detail. Often people will bullet point what they are grateful for like:

- My house
- My phone
- My bed
- My dinner

But this is a lifeless list with zero emotion attached to it. You need to *feel* grateful. Give yourself emotion-triggering detail. Your brain likes and responds best to exciting descriptive words! For example:

> I am so grateful for my cozy home. I always feel extremely safe in it. It keeps me warm when it's cold outside and protects me from the wind and rain. I love how I have decorated my bedroom and how calming it is to relax here. I'm really excited to decorate the living room next! I'm so lucky to have my own space. I am so thankful.

Then read over your own words and *feel* the gratitude you poured onto the page.

The Power of Visualization

Visualization is also an extremely powerful mindset-shifting technique. If you have ever experienced having a panic attack, you know that it often starts with imagining something negative. If we reverse this fact, then it makes sense that visualizing positive things will have a positive effect.

Just as I guided you to imagine the best parts of your day each evening, you can extend this visualization and imagine your best day ever.

Visualization is best done before we sleep or just as we wake up because our minds are in the most relaxed state. This is a similar state to hypnosis, which makes the visualization even more effective. Whatever your absolute dreamiest, most successful, happiest, best day is, imagine it!

→ WRITE IT DOWN: Change How You See Yourself

Keeping in mind your inner child, your ability to control your thoughts, and the prompt to challenge your perceptions, I want you to write down all the wonderful things about yourself—every positive trait you feel you have, including those related to ADHD.

It's okay if you feel some resistance when you're doing this. This is your wounded self feeling a sense of injustice. You're challenging the victim mindset as you do this, and it may feel untruthful at first.

The number one rule for this practice: you must pretend that the child version of yourself is going to read what you have written. Your goal here is not to lie to yourself but to solely focus on all your positives.

Begin with "I see myself as someone who . . ." Here's an example to get you started:

> I see myself as someone who deeply cares about others. I like to laugh, sing, and dance around my kitchen. My thoughts can create such vivid images, and I think really quickly! I . . ."

Any time a negative thought about yourself comes to mind, you can think about this journal entry, so make sure it is filled to the brim with positive evidence of your wonderful self!

→ WRITE IT DOWN: Rewrite Your Story

This is the most powerful part of your perspective reset. This practice takes each negatively perceived part of your life and shifts it into something you no longer feel holds you back or negatively impacts you. In best-case scenarios, you can even come to an eventual feeling of gratitude for some of your negatively perceived experiences.

Go through these sentences to form a picture of your life with a new perspective. Each sentence starts by giving a summary of the situation we have negatively perceived. Write the negative experience as a statement. For example:

> "I was diagnosed with ADHD and couldn't get any professional support."

We then continue this with:

> "If that didn't happen, I would never have. . ."

You then complete the sentence with everything positive that this caused. Repeat "I would never have" as many times as you need to, solely focusing on any positive outcome. Here's mine:

> I was diagnosed with ADHD and couldn't get any professional support. If that didn't happen, I would never have understood my mind. I would never have looked into symptom management tools and become fascinated with the topic. I would never have spoken out on social media and built a community I am so connected to. I would never have developed the emotional intelligence I have today that helps with every single relationship I have. I would never have written a book on the topic to help others. I would never have . . .

Finally, if you feel you can, finish your reframing practice with gratitude. This is mine:

> I am so grateful to have received an ADHD diagnosis and not been given any professional support.

You don't need to do this for every single one of your negatively perceived experiences right now. But try to do at least one right now.

Resistance Is Part of the Process When You Change How You See Yourself

As we work through the rest of your ADHD reset, wounded parts of yourself may present themselves. Often these parts are connected to a negative situation that impacted you that you still hold on to. In those moments, try to do the Rewrite Your Story practice.

Every person whom I've worked with feels some resistance during the process. This is because their subconscious beliefs are in conflict with their new story. Another major factor to our thoughts is our belief system. You'll learn more about this in the next chapter.

→ REFLECT AND ACT: Affirm Your Positive Mindset

If you feel you need to add in even more positive thinking, you can use positive affirmations. They are short, uplifting statements that reinforce positive beliefs about yourself and your abilities.

Here are some tailored affirmations to support having ADHD:

- I embrace my unique way of thinking.
- I am worthy of love and acceptance just as I am.
- I focus on progress, not perfection.
- I have the power to choose my thoughts and actions.
- I love myself.
- (Add in your own here.)

Write these affirmations on sticky notes or pieces of paper and stick them in places where you will see and read them daily. A common successful place to put them is on your bathroom mirror so you can read them to yourself as you brush your teeth.

The Most Important Things You Need to Know

- Our thoughts directly impact how we feel and the actions we choose to take. Your thoughts truly do become your reality!
- Your current negative perceptions can be challenged and changed with mindful thinking.
- Practicing gratitude is proven to increase your overall well-being.
- Connecting to your inner child gives you a perspective shift on how you talk to yourself. If you wouldn't say it to little you, don't say it to grown-up you!
- If a negative situation comes to mind and you quickly want to redirect your thoughts, you can prompt yourself by saying, "If that didn't happen, I would never have . . ."

Battle of the Beliefs:

Letting Go of Limits and the Lies You Tell Yourself

EVERYONE HAS A SET OF CORE BELIEFS that rule our way of being. The actions you take, who you befriend, the jobs you choose, the decisions you make are all based on your beliefs. The problem is that we aren't always consciously aware of what our beliefs are, and many can be negative beliefs that limit us unconsciously!

Our beliefs begin to form at a very young age, starting in early childhood and continuing to develop throughout our lives. Our foundational beliefs are formed and solidified between birth and age twelve; and they are often subconscious, ingrained in our way of being. That's why you feel resistance when you try to change them.

You begin to form your own core beliefs in your adolescence (13 to 18 years), based on what you learn from your parents, your teachers, the world around you, and your own observations. Often these beliefs are easier to identify and change because you were more aware of them as they were being formed. You took a more active role in deciding whether you wanted to keep these beliefs and live by them.

Your adulthood beliefs develop due to new experiences and further life lessons. What's interesting is that at any age, you are always expanding from your *original* foundational beliefs (0 to 12 years) if they have been left unchallenged and unaltered.

How Different Beliefs Create How We See the World

Conscious beliefs: These are beliefs that you are aware of. You could easily tell some-one about it if asked to give an example of one of these beliefs—for example, "I believe that mental health matters." Conscious beliefs are formed through conscious thought, learning, evaluation of evidence, and your personal experiences. For example, you may believe that regular exercise is good for your health through what you have been taught and see to be logically true. You can easily change conscious beliefs through logical thinking, such as outgrowing your belief in Santa Claus or fairies. But just in case, "I do believe in fairies. I do, I do!"

Subconscious beliefs: These beliefs exist below the level of conscious awareness. They are formed through repeated experiences, conditioning, and internalization of messages from various sources such as family, friends, society, and culture. These beliefs can influence your thoughts, emotions, behaviors, and perceptions without your conscious awareness! For example, you may hold a subconscious belief that speaking your mind is rude because you felt people reacted negatively when you were outspoken as a child. No one even had to directly tell you, "Children should be seen and not heard, especially if they have ADHD." This is something you have subconsciously absorbed and believe, and you have adjusted your behavior accordingly.

Limiting subconscious beliefs: These are subconscious beliefs that hinder your per-sonal growth, success, and well-being. They are negative in nature. They can create barriers throughout life and result in you not living up to your full potential. Limiting beliefs often bubble up as negative thoughts such as "I'm not good enough," "I can't do it," or "They are better than me."

Here is a visual to show you the flow of how we witness or experience something, form a belief based on that, and then have new thoughts because of the belief we have formed.

Interestingly, we also create a feedback loop to reinforce the belief and actively try to seek *more* experiences that further cement the belief to be true!

The visual below shows that when we experience something, we form a belief, but that's not all. We also create thoughts that feed back into that belief. As we move through life, we look for confirmation of this belief that proves it to be true. This is called confirmation bias.

Change Your Beliefs, Change Your Thoughts, Change Your Life

So, we're going to focus on your limiting subconscious beliefs and break these damaging feedback loops. Limiting beliefs can stop you from fully transforming your perception, mindset, and life for the better. Negative experiences, external events, conditioning, and internalized messages have become part of you. But it isn't you, and trust me, you can break free.

It is normal to have a set of limiting beliefs. It is nature's way of trying to help us make sense of the world and ourselves. It's not exclusive to ADHD. However, I can guarantee that most of us with ADHD have plenty of limiting beliefs that developed because we felt different and may have been treated differently. Our differences may even have been pointed out to us as a bad thing! Sadly we are often told untruths or even lies, but our subconscious mind accepts the nonfactual as fact, especially if it comes from a parent or authority figure, such as a teacher.

My Experience with Limiting Beliefs

When I was a little girl, my family would always tell me how cute I was. Being called pretty was a common compliment I would receive, and so I believed myself to be pretty. But one day at school when I was eight years old, a boy called me fat and ugly. I didn't feel upset or angry. I felt completely confused, like a total fraud, for the rest of the day. Everything we are told at this vital age is absorbed as fact. My brain couldn't compute how the two statements could both be true!

Obviously, as an adult, I can now use my critical thinking and dismiss the bully's remarks. But it wasn't said to me as an adult. It was said to me during the period of my life when my foundational beliefs were being formed and solidified!

When I returned home, I sat in front of my bedroom mirror and looked at myself with a deep adultlike frown: "Am I ugly?" My brain quickly gave me all the evidence to prove it not to be true, but then it did something it hadn't done before: it found all the evidence to prove what he said *was* true.

Our brain does this because negative information tends to be more salient; it stands out to us and is more memorable than positive information. This is known as negativity bias. The negative comments, especially from peers at a young age, can be emotionally distressing, which makes them more impactful than compliments and harder to ignore. It was the first time in my life that I felt ugly, but it was never going to be the last. My brain would now search for evidence of it being true. My new belief, "I am fat and ugly," was formed.

Limiting beliefs can actually be formed to try to protect us. Each limiting belief aims to avoid pain and discomfort and maintain stability and preserve our self-concept. Self-concept is how you see and understand yourself, including your beliefs, feelings, and thoughts about your abilities, appearance , values, and personality.

In my case, I was protecting my self-concept by altering how I perceived myself so that the conflicting remarks didn't feel like a threat to my sense of self. I accepted my new identity as "fat and ugly" to avoid the uncomfortable feeling of being a fraud, masquerading around as a pretty little girl when "in fact" I wasn't (according to the interaction with the bully, which created my limiting belief).

ADHD 101: Examples of How Our Limiting Beliefs Try to Protect Us

- Avoiding pain and discomfort
    - "I can't succeed" shields us from disappointment.
    - "I'm not good enough" protects us from emotional hurt.
- Maintaining stability and predictability
    - "It's too risky" avoids uncertain situations.
    - "Change is bad" keeps life stable.
- Preserving self-concept
    - "This is who I am" maintains our self-identity.
    - "I must be consistent" helps maintain a clear and stable self-identity.
- Managing expectations
    - "I shouldn't aim too high" prevents disappointment.
    - "I shouldn't get my hopes up" shields us from emotional pain.

These mechanisms, while protective, often hinder personal growth. Recognizing and challenging limiting beliefs can lead to more empowering beliefs that support our goals and well-being.

We want to fit in and feel accepted by the peers, which can make us accept and internalize negative feedback, even if it harms our self-esteem. Paradoxically, believing the negative feedback can protect our feelings by aligning our self-perception with the feedback, reducing its emotional impact and discomfort if we hear it again.

Through the years, this has been a recurring limiting belief for me that's impacted my life in negative ways. It reduced my confidence, lowered my self-worth, and made me feel inferior to others. The bully's initial remark resulted in more negative self-talk that also impacted my self-esteem years later. This false belief became so ingrained in me and the neural pathways of my brain that negative self-talk became my default.

Battle of the Beliefs

If you're like me, when you try to override your negative thoughts, perceptions, and actions, you can hit what feels like a brick wall. Because you are! Limiting beliefs stop us from acting or thinking in more positive ways. That's because these new thoughts are in direct conflict with the negative ways we have seen ourselves or our lives. Endless repetition of negative thoughts blaze a path in our brain.

It's difficult to create a new path with new beliefs when they would be in direct conflict with what you already believe. It can almost feel impossible to let go of your negative thought patterns because they are attached to a subconscious limiting belief that will not accept being proved wrong!

Why Negative Subconscious Beliefs Are So Stubborn

Our subconscious beliefs *believe* they are fact. They are like an annoying, arrogant old man, stuck in his ways, trying to convince you that the world was a better place when women were treated as second-class citizens. Your logical conscious brain is telling the old geezer (your subconscious limiting belief), "Listen here, that is not factual at all," but he waves his hand in a dismissing way and arrogantly says, "I am right, you are wrong." That is what our limiting belief system acts like, which is exactly why saying affirmations alone will not work!

I could repeat a new belief—"I am beautiful"—to myself every day, but the inner old arrogant jerk can wave these affirmations aside easily. So how do we finally rid ourselves of these untrue limiting beliefs and form new healthy beliefs?

The Cycle: How Limiting Beliefs and Thoughts Make You Feel Bad

Let's take a look at how our beliefs control us in your everyday life. Once you realize that many of your thoughts, emotions, and actions are being controlled by your subconscious beliefs, you will actively want to change them!

This graphic shows you how our subconscious limiting beliefs not only create the thoughts we have but also trigger our emotions and alter what actions we take!

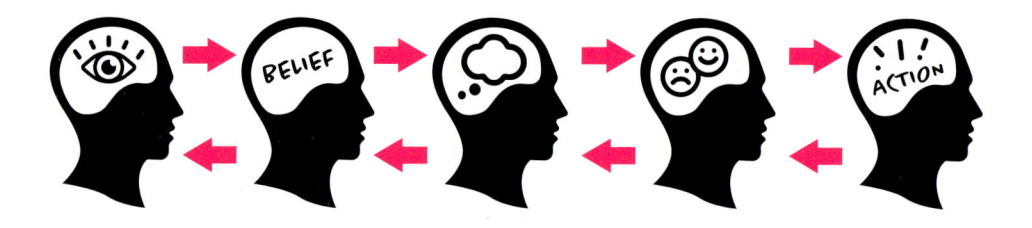

For example, based on my old limiting *belief* of being ugly,
- → I would often *think*, "I am disgusting" or "I'm so ugly."
- → These thoughts would make me *feel* sad.
- → I would then *act* on this feeling and decide to wear something very plain in an attempt to cover my body and avoid drawing attention to myself no matter where I was going.
- → This *action* would then influence how I was feeling: insecure,
- → Which reinforced my negative *mood* because I didn't feel good in what I was wearing.
- → I would have more negative *thoughts* about myself, such as "I look awful."
- → These thoughts fed back into the existing *belief*, and I would be on the *lookout* for any evidence to prove it to be true while I was at the event, further reinforcing the belief.

Then the cycle starts again with an even more ingrained limiting belief, and this happens constantly!

This is why I am a solid believer in the logical sense of "Thoughts turn into things." They do, every single day. We are navigated by our thoughts and base our actions on them, which in turn creates the lives we live.

Stop Self-Sabotage

I know that sometimes it feels like you are your own worst enemy. Beliefs and fears can cause us to sabotage our own efforts, and we feel pretty sucky about it, blaming ourselves and damaging our self-trust along the way. I want you to feel completely comforted in this moment. *You are not your own worst enemy.*

Our brain has been trying to protect us by keeping our core subconscious beliefs safe to avoid inner conflict between our beliefs and self-concept. Unfortunately, our brain doesn't realize that some of our beliefs outright suck and the actions we have been trying to take would massively benefit us!

How many times in the past have you wanted to take a new positive action but chose the old negative action? There are several reasons for this, including our executive function, which I'll cover later in the book, and when our beliefs conflict with new actions we want to take. But don't worry, I'm here to help you.

ADHD: Keeping It Simple

What Is Self-Sabotage?
Self-sabotage is when individuals hinder their own success and well-being through negative behaviors. It's when you unknowingly trip yourself up or stand in your own way, and it often comes from a mix of the following causes:

Causes
- Limiting beliefs: negative beliefs that make us play small
- Low self-esteem: feeling unworthy of success
- Fear of failure or success: avoiding risks and new responsibilities
- Comfort zones: staying in familiar patterns to avoid discomfort
- Past trauma: negative experiences that shape current behaviors

Overcoming Self-Sabotage
- Self-awareness: Recognize and understand your behaviors.
- Challenge negative beliefs: Replace them with positive, empowering ones.
- Set realistic goals: Break tasks into manageable steps.
- Develop coping strategies: Find healthy ways to manage stress.
- Practice self-compassion: Be kind to yourself and forgive mistakes.

Imagine yourself in four different ways:

1. Your body is the ship.
2. Your limiting beliefs are the ocean.
3. Your limiting thoughts are the crew.
4. Your conscious mind is the captain.

When you self-sabotage, by not taking positive new action, ocean water (your limiting beliefs) seeps onto the deck of the ship (your body). The captain (your conscious mind) who wanted to navigate you to calmer water falls overboard, so the crew (your limiting thoughts) decides what path to take. But this leads you into more troubled waters! You need to rescue the captain so they can take back control of your ship!

Think about a moment you wanted to do something positive but didn't do it. Perhaps you were sitting on the sofa toying with the idea of going for a run. Putting executive dysfunction to the side for now, what else came into play here? Negative thoughts? Limiting beliefs? Ask yourself if the captain, your conscious mind, was navigating you. Or had the ship been taken over by the crew (your negative thoughts) and rocky waters (your limiting beliefs)?

How to Take Back Control of Your Ship

The next time you feel resistance to something you consciously want to do, such as going for a walk instead of scrolling on your phone, tell your crew who the captain is. Literally talk to your crew: "Hey! I am the captain, and this is what we are doing!" Then take control and sail yourself to your positive destination.

Doing this regularly short-circuits the negative limiting-belief feedback loops in your brain. It stops negative self-talk, helps you move past any resistance you feel, and over-rides limiting beliefs that can make you miserable. The more you do this, the more your unruly crew will start to listen to you!

Remember, you can also disrupt habitual negative thoughts by:

1. Recognize the thought is negative.
2. Stop the negative thought process.
3. Say "I'm sorry" and something kind ("I love you") while you picture your inner child.

→ WRITE IT DOWN: How to Pinpoint Your Limiting Beliefs

You can make your subconscious beliefs conscious by noticing how you talk about yourself. Do you use negative "I am" statements, such as "I am stupid," "I am not good enough," "I am too much"? These are all limiting beliefs.

Write down three of your most common recurring negative "I am" statements.

Next, look at your first statement and ask yourself, "Who or what made me feel this way for the very first time?"

Take your time with this practice. Let your mind wander back in time. If a recent scenario comes up, acknowledge that this added to the limiting belief but continue asking, "When was the very first time?"

This is exactly how I remembered the boy at school when I was eight years old and pinpointed the exact moment I first felt ugly when looking in a mirror.

Why Is It important to Find Out What Formed the Belief?

When we take ourselves back to the first moment in our past when we adopted a limiting belief, we are often able to see that it's based on a lie, wasn't deserved, and shouldn't have defined us. This realization increases our empathy and self-love because we no longer want to continue feeding the limiting negative belief. We look back from a higher self-perspective and define the moment differently, based on the truth. It disempowers the limiting belief.

Your new perspective helps you detach from the limiting belief. You'll see that the person you were when the belief was formed is not the person you are today. This self-awareness and understanding will help you recognize the next time a limiting belief shows up in your life and enable you to dismiss it as being untrue.

Healing can happen when we understand why we feel negatively about ourselves. Here's how.

→ WRITE IT DOWN: Fact over Fiction

We're going to take your limiting beliefs to court. You must act as your own lawyer, using the truth as your defense. The jury must agree with you that the limiting belief you have put on trial is a lie that needs to be abolished!

In your journal, write an "I am" statement in quotation marks. For example: "I am stupid." Following this, write "I object!"

Then convince the jury why this is a total lie, a complete fiction, providing them with every bit of factual evidence you can drum up. For example:

> I am able to read and write, learn new skills, and teach others things that I know. If a subject interests me, I spend hours in hyperfocus, learning everything about the subject. I was told that I was stupid when I was seven years old, because I got a math question wrong, but that does not mean I am a stupid person. It means I didn't have the answer to one math question at a very young age. I am extremely emotionally intelligent. I recognize when others' moods shift when no one else notices. I can keep a conversation going with total ease . . .

Continue writing as much evidence as you can, then finish the argument with a positive "I am" statement that uses an exciting descriptive word. Our brains latch on a little better when we do this! Example: "I am *amazingly* clever."

This can work as a new affirmation that you say daily to begin wiring in new positive beliefs without any conflict!

Abolish the Belief

Next, cross out your original negative "I am" statement until it is unreadable and no longer exists on the page. You can even cut out this section of the page and dispose of the statement if you'd like. Whatever feels best for you.

Then I would like you to sit back and imagine someone telling you, "You are a giraffe," and without hesitation you calmly say, "No, I am not." Imagine yourself laughing about it. Feel your confidence in this moment. Notice how ridiculous it feels to you. Maintain that emotion and let the imaginary person say your abolished "I am" statement and reply in exactly the same way—with calm confidence and a sense of its untrue ridiculousness: "No, I am not."

Finish with your new opposing "I am" statement. For example: "No, I am not. I am amazingly clever!"

You can go over this process for every limiting belief that reveals itself to you.

Now you can see that you have been unknowingly telling yourself negative lies all your life! It's time to start telling yourself the truth!

→ FIVE-MINUTE RESET: Be Present

You have reflected a lot during this chapter. Let's bring you back to the now with a quick interactive practice. In your mind, answer the following questions:

- What page number of the book are you on right now?
- How are you holding the book? Are you using one hand? Both?
- Are you standing up, seated, or lying down?
- Where are you right now? What room? In what location?
- What can you hear right now?

Take a few deep breaths and pull in the oxygen that surrounds you. Adjust your body to feel comfortable and continue on with the present moment.

The Most Important Things You Need to Know

- As children, we absorb everything as fact, which is why we can have extremely untruthful limiting beliefs about ourselves as adults.
- Our subconscious limiting beliefs do not like to be proven wrong. We have to actively come into conflict and override them until they no longer rule us.
- Your beliefs trigger what thoughts you have. Your thoughts trigger your emotions. Your emotions impact the actions you decide to take. This all means your beliefs create the life you live.
- You are the captain! Consciously demand your mind to sail in the direction you desire!

Tell Yourself Better Lies:
Becoming Who You Want to Be

I WOULD LOVE TO TELL YOU that once you prove your limiting beliefs to be untrue, they disappear. Unfortunately, the associated neural pathways created by negative self-talk still live in your mind, and making them fully redundant is a gradual process. I am going to offer you something very special now that will work wonders—a hypnosis script!

How Hypnosis Helps to Rewire Your Mind

Hypnosis is a state of focused attention and increased suggestibility that can help you change your thoughts, behaviors, perceptions, and beliefs! It's not standing on a stage while a hypnotist makes you cluck like a chicken!

Hypnosis and guided meditation are similar processes. They both provide relaxing experiences simply through listening, and you are always in full control. So, don't worry. During hypnosis, the brain shifts into alpha waves (relaxed but alert) and theta waves (deep relaxation and light sleep). This state helps access the subconscious and supports making positive changes.

Hypnosis enables you to:

- Bypass the critical conscious mind and access the subconscious where your deep-seated beliefs are.
- Access a state of enhanced suggestibility, which can help implant new positive beliefs, thoughts, and behaviors.
- Break negative patterns by interrupting and reframing negative thought patterns; and introducing you to new healthier ways of thinking, reinforcing new neural pathways.
- Adjust memory and perception by helping you reframe past experiences, altering how you perceive and react to them.
- Reduce stress and anxiety by promoting relaxation, which makes it even easier to adopt new thoughts and behaviors!

DIY Hypnosis: Yes, It Really Works!

Hypnosis is usually done one-on-one or via a personalized recording by a professional hypnotherapist. But let me tell you a little secret. You can put yourself into a hypnotic state that will help you change your thoughts and your life.

You'll do this by recording the script that I've provided on page 88. This is an adaptation of the script I've used with clients and myself to help release limiting beliefs. The most recent limiting belief I released for myself was "It's so hard to make money." Since releasing this belief and implanting new positive beliefs, I feel confident, I find work much easier, and I believe I can make money with ease. Gone are the days that I over-work and overcomplicate my work! This belief-release script will act as a DIY version of this powerful work.

Record yourself reading this script on your phone and play this every evening before bed for a minimum of thirty days. When recording yourself, read slowly, calmly, and with a soothing neutral tone.

How to Practice DIY Hypnosis

Focus your hypnosis sessions on one limiting belief at a time. Don't cram everything into one! Your brain is working hard, and you don't want to overload it.

If you are torn between which limiting belief you would like to fully release first, answer this question: If I waved a magic wand in front of you and could make a limiting belief vanish, which would you like me to cast away? *That's* the one to start with!

If you have resistance to this practice, that's okay. I did too, before having my own hypnosis sessions and studying hypnotherapy. I felt anxious when I drove and thought hypnosis wouldn't work to calm that anxiety. I proclaimed, "I'm not suggestible. This won't work." But guess what? It did! Thirty days later, I no longer felt anxious when driving. Worst-case scenario, this hypnosis practice will help you sleep better. So, believe me, you have nothing to lose other than the limiting belief you want to let go of!

→ **BELIEF RELEASE: Your Script to Release Limiting Beliefs**

Please do not listen to this recording while driving or when you need to be fully alert. You are about to enter into a very relaxed state. You love listening to this hypnosis recording that you made for yourself. It proves to you that you are actively helping yourself let go of limiting beliefs that no longer serve you. Listening to this recording is an important part of your nighttime routine that you love and *really* look forward to every day.

[*Pause*]

Now, [*your name,*] let yourself relax. Feel free to move around until you are in a comfortable and rested position. Once you are relaxed, take a long, slow, deep breath in and out, and find your natural steady breathing pace. Feel your body resting on your bed and let the energy from the day fall away.

[*Pause*]

As you go deeper into a totally relaxed state, you are aware of a wonderful transformation taking place in your personality. You understand the power of hypnosis and that it is the most liberating and transformative power. You are going to listen to this with your subconscious mind with total trust and excitement for the transformation taking place. You know that hypnosis is extremely transformative.

You know that you are incredibly suggestible. You know that hypnosis bypasses your conscious mind and directly speaks to your subconscious. Your beliefs are yours to change, and this recording is helping you to make changes that will benefit you for the rest of your life.

[*Pause*]

You understand something even more powerful: When you were a young child, you formed limiting beliefs that were untrue, and now your beliefs are yours to transform. You are transforming them right now. You believe with unwavering certainty that as an adult, it is not necessary for you to hold on to the old limiting beliefs that you used to believe or to think the negative thoughts that you thought then. Your past self, the person who formed the limiting beliefs, is most definitely not you now. It is the past. It is behind you. It's something you used to believe. It cannot, will not, does not ever affect you again. [*Your name,*] you are free now.

[*Pause*]

Tonight, while you rest, your mind will let go of the old belief you had of [*say the limiting belief; example: "being a failure"*]. You let go of this right *now*! You have proven this belief is untrue.

In fact, you have proven that you now believe the total opposite. You believe [*say the new empowering belief; example: "You are a success!"*]. You believe this with total certainty.

This is your real empowering belief, and every time you feel your new powerful and positive belief, the old limiting belief fades further and further away until it is no longer in your mind at all. It is gone. You have let go of this old limiting belief. Now that you believe [*say the new empowering belief*], you feel more confident.

You feel mentally stronger.
You feel happier.
You feel [*add more feelings that work with your new belief*].

[*Pause*]

You are free to [*add something that you wouldn't have done before; example: take chances on yourself*] and be your authentic, wonderful self.

[*Pause*]

As you accept these suggestions, your amazing, talented mind is empowering you to form better, stronger, and positive beliefs that will transform your life for the better.

You are confident.
You are calm.
You are likeable.
You are loved.

You have let go of the past. You feel fantastic about the present, and you are excited about your future. You have no limits.

[*Pause*]

As you feel this newfound freedom, you can sleep peacefully knowing that this recording continues to reorganize your subconscious mind to work for you in the best way possible.

This recording should be three to five minutes long, depending on your pace. What I love most about this transformative work is that it is effortless! Once you have the recording, you just hit play and close your eyes. It is the easiest kind of mindset work you will ever do!

Tell Yourself Better Lies

I felt an inner conflict when I first tried the hypnosis and affirmation methods. To me it felt like I was attempting to tell myself a bunch of lies because I was so heavily attached to the untruths of my subconscious limiting beliefs. Let me reframe this for you. You can tell yourself better lies!

The new positive thoughts and beliefs you are trying to rewire into your mind may not feel honest to you right now. Challenging my belief that "I am a failure" by telling my brain "I am a great success" just felt icky to me. However, over time, these "better lies" transitioned to finally feeling like the truth that they are. Since I decided to let in the belief of being a success, I have become a success!

You have spent years feeding your mind utter BS beliefs and letting your inner voice repeat negative things to yourself. Why not feed your mind positive BS beliefs that make your mind think powerful thoughts, have positive emotions, and trigger great actions?

Your Voice Is Powerful

As you've learned, your inner voice is important, but so is your outer voice—the things you say out loud throughout the day without much thought. It's very common for someone with ADHD to mask their insecurities by announcing perceived flaws and limiting beliefs.

I always know when a limiting belief is lingering in my subconscious because I will casually voice them. When I say things out loud like "I suck at this so bad," my inner negative thoughts and emotions increase, and my actions reflect that.

Take a moment to think about the things you say about yourself out loud either to yourself or others.

- Do you make negative jokes about yourself often?
- Do you openly judge yourself in front of others?
- Do you say negative statements about yourself?
- Do you ever look for evidence from those around you to prove it to be true?

Consider how you feel after these moments of self-deprecation. Insecure? Unworthy? Unhappy? That's how powerful our spoken words are. They have a huge inner impact. The good news is that we can flip this script! From now on, you're going to regularly vocalize positive and powerful statements and kick to the curb the confident critic who has been sharing your one-star rating!

The Power of Projected Affirmations

Saying nice things about ourselves can make us feel uncomfortable and even trigger a fear of appearing arrogant and possibly being rejected. It's much easier to project positive affirmations away from yourself and onto someone else, because being kind to others doesn't trigger negative judgments by others.

So, it makes sense to start working with affirmations by giving compliments to others. This will help you begin the journey of using your powerful voice to improve your outer and inner critic. Plus, our subconscious mind listens to *everything*. It doesn't filter if we are saying these things about ourselves or someone else, so we'll absorb the positivity from what we say to others on a subconscious level!

For this to work best, try to make affirmations feel as natural as possible. It's actually pretty easy. Here are some examples of projected affirmations you can say out loud to others:

To a Friend
- "I believe in you! You can do this!"
- "You are more than capable and can achieve this."
- "You have a wonderful positive energy."

To a Family Member
- "I really appreciate everything you do for our family."
- "You are a really important part of my life."
- "You have always inspired me."

To a Colleague
- "I am always impressed with how hard you work."
- "You bring so much value to this team."
- "You really make a big difference."

To Your Partner
- "I love you just the way you are."
- "You make my life better."
- "I'm grateful for you every day."

To a Child
- "I am so proud of you and the person you are becoming."
- "You are loved just as you are, no matter what."
- "You are so smart!"

To a Mentor or Teacher
- "Your guidance has a huge impact on my life."
- "I admire how much knowledge you have."
- "Thank you for believing in me."

If these feel too bold for your starting point, that is fine. Simplify your projected affirmations until they flow out as casual compliments.

Positive Self-Talk Is Good for Others and Good for Us

Think about it. What we notice and value in others often reflects what we value in ourselves. Speaking about others with love and kindness is a true reflection of our own inner love and kindness. The more you do this for others, the easier it is going to become to speak nicely about yourself. Eventually you can start integrating positive self-talk into your daily life too. Here are some spoken affirmations that you can say about yourself to others as your confidence grows:

To a Friend
- "I'm learning to accept myself for who I am, and it feels great."
- "I'm really proud of myself for X."
- "I've dealt with some tough situations, but I've realized just how strong I am."

To a Family Member
- "I deserve to be loved by others like I love you."
- "I'm trying to practice gratitude more, and I feel really grateful for my life."
- "I think younger me would be proud of what I am doing."

To a Colleague
- "I work really hard and take pride in what I do."
- "I am really proud of what I have been working on."
- "I see myself getting better at this every day."

To Your Partner
- "I'm learning to love myself more, and it's making our relationship stronger."
- "After going through that together, I realize how resilient I am."
- "I'm a better person than when we met because I am always growing."

To a Mentor or Teacher
- "Your guidance has helped me grow so much. I am always striving to improve."
- "I have gained a lot more confidence in my abilities."
- "Looking back at where I started, I am really proud of where I am now."

Using these in-conversation affirmations will help you reinforce your new positive mindset and diminish your limiting beliefs. You will also find that those around you, if they're positive people, will welcome and return your affirmations to you, further reinforcing this part of your mindset reset.

If you feel someone's resistance to your kindness or it isn't returned, that is completely normal. As a society, we have sadly normalized negative conversation, dismissing compliments and putting ourselves down. Don't let it deter you. This is proof that your positivity is needed in the world!

Review Your Highlights Reel

In addition to listening to your hypnosis tape, I encourage you to adopt another evening ritual. Every evening, practice "telling yourself better lies" or review your highlights reel.

This reel is composed of your best moments, similar to what you'd see at the end of a reality TV competition—a montage of the highlights and best bits from the season. You can do this by replaying your day in your mind and focusing on every little positive moment. Review everything from the small win of not forgetting to brush your teeth that morning to something you saw on social media that made you smile to laughing with someone at work—anything that feels positive to you upon reflection.

Once you're done, ask yourself, "So, what does the future look like for you now?" (Just like a game show asks the competitors.) This is your turn to visualize your next day exactly as you want it to unfold. Make sure you don't turn this into a long list of to-dos. Instead, visualize the highlights of the new day as you'd like them to happen naturally. After you do this powerful visualization practice, begin your hypnosis recording. This is such a healthy and positive way to enter into a deep relaxing sleep, and it takes you one step closer to becoming the version of yourself that you want to be.

Be Real with Yourself and Rebuild Self Trust

Earlier I explained the damage that can be caused by the lies we tell ourselves when we engage in negative self-talk and how we can transform these moments by telling ourselves better lies. This includes changing thoughts such as "I can't do it" to "I *can* do it!" simply by choosing healthier thoughts, even if they don't feel truthful in the moment. Now we are going to look at a different set of lies that can only be combated by being real with yourself!

A common limiting belief among the ADHD community is that of being a quitter—someone who has failed at many things, who is unreliable and inconsistent. This theme of self-doubt and lack of confidence often stems from past experiences where ADHD-related challenges made success difficult to achieve.

To combat this, you might overpromise and overcommit, leading to burnout and reinforcing the belief that you're a quitter. You create impossible to-do lists and set outrageously large goals without any structure, effectively not being honest with yourself. While having big dreams is admirable, it's crucial to be real about what's realistically achievable in your day-to-day tasks and goals.

If I plan to go to the gym, I need to be absolutely certain that I will follow through, or I don't commit to it at all. To say "I'll go to the gym later" and then fail to go creates a moment of disappointment, reinforcing the belief that "I am a quitter."

I don't want you to adopt an "I won't do it anyway" attitude. Instead, I want you to challenge yourself and question if you'll actually follow through. Disappointing yourself with this kind of lie is more damaging than being realistic about your expectations for the day.

We will revisit this later in the book, but it's important to see the power of our words—to understand when positive self-talk helps versus when overcommitting hinders. It's crucial to know when to feed our subconscious something aspirational, such as "I am successful," versus setting ourselves up for disappointment with unrealistic promises, such as "I will clean the *entire* house today." Instead of feeling proud of cleaning one room, the overpromise turns a potential victory into a disappointment.

These unrealistic expectations that you may fail to achieve build up until you can no longer trust your own word. Rebuilding this trust in yourself is vital to becoming your own trustworthy best friend.

→ MINDSET RESET: Gratitude

Answer the following questions and feel grateful for each answer:

- What is something that made you smile this week?
- Who made you laugh recently?
- What was a win (big or small) for you this month?
- What item do you use every single day that makes your life easier?

The Most Important Things You Need to Know

- Hypnosis is a relaxed state of mind that increases suggestibility so that you are able to change your thoughts, behaviors, perceptions, and beliefs with ease.
- You are always still in full control when in a hypnotic state. You are able to hear and react to alarms, notifications, and anyone entering the room.
- Using the projected affirmation method is a great place to start when shifting your thoughts from negative to positive because we often find it more comfortable to say kind things to others than we do ourselves.
- Affirmations in conversation help you reinforce your new positive thoughts about yourself, speeding up the process of this part of your mindset reset.
- Overpromising often leads to disappointment instead of creating moments of self-pride. Be honest with what you are able to achieve on a case-by-case basis.

Become Your Own Best Friend:
Healing Your Relationship with Self

THINKING OF YOURSELF AS YOUR OWN BEST FRIEND can feel uncomfortable. Maybe it even sounds a little lonely and desperate to you, if you have never been encouraged to treat yourself as your very own bestie. Becoming your own best friend isn't based on how many friends you have or how often you socialize. It isn't about others at all. It is all about you and your loving relationship with self.

The opposite of love is usually described as hate, but I beg to differ. Hate at least comes with passion, emotion, and being hurt because you do in fact feel love underneath all that pain. The opposite of love, in my opinion, is indifference. Indifference is when you don't care; you feel dull, muted, and nothing particularly excites or bothers you. It is not joy, sadness, or anger but rather a lack of feeling altogether. It is a flatline of emotions.

If you resonate with feelings of self-hate, I am going to show you how to push past that pain barrier and discover the unconditional love living underneath. If you have propelled yourself to the opposite of self-love and feel indifferent toward yourself, I will help you reignite the lowly lit flame until it is roaring again!

Self-Love Matters

Self-love and being your own best friend isn't self-indulgence. It's self-preservation in this challenging world. No one told us that growing up with ADHD can damage our relationship with self, but our ADHD community definitely proves that it can do just that.

It's likely that you put more pressure on yourself in school than your peers did. You also probably felt frustrated and disappointed with yourself, embarrassed, confused, and rejected—more than your peers. Eventually you become your very own bully instead of your best friend.

For me, the self-love manuals I read in young adulthood felt a little too surface level for the relationship breakdown I had experienced and needed to heal. A self-loving mantra and face mask just wasn't going to cut it!

Your feelings of self-frustration, self-doubt, and insecurity are all valid. You have been expected to flawlessly navigate a neurotypical world with a neurodivergent brain. That is a lot of pressure. You likely weren't taught that you needed to be patient with yourself; that you needed to practice unconditional love and understanding throughout your life to avoid slipping into the pits of perfectionism and self-loathing.

The mask you wore so very tightly to conceal all your felt flaws and differences means that you swallowed down and internalized failure every time you felt you didn't do something quite right. You didn't understand what the teacher said when everyone else did—swallow. You forgot your friend's birthday present even though you put it right by your door—swallow. You missed the appointment—swallow. You ignored the dishes— swallow. You couldn't keep up—swallow, swallow, swallow! It becomes internalized and manifests as a lack of self-**belief**, self-**care**, and self-**trust**.

If a friend repeatedly said "I don't **believe** in you," would you think that friend was good for you? If a best friend were to say "I don't **care** about you," would you want them by your side when you did something you care about? If your bestie said "I don't **trust** you because you made mistakes," would you be okay with that or would you think that they are a total judgmental jerk? Guess what? This is what you often say to yourself!

ADHD 101: Do You Have a Damaged Relationship with Yourself?

Here are fourteen signs of a damaged relationship with self:

1. **Lack of self-trust**
   - Difficulty believing in your own decisions and constant second-guessing
2. **Low self-esteem**
   - Persistent feelings of inadequacy and worthlessness
3. **Self-sabotage**
   - Behaviors that undermine your success and well-being
   - Procrastination and avoidance of opportunities
4. **Negative self-talk**
   - Internal dialogue filled with criticism and negativity
   - Difficulty accepting compliments or positive feedback
5. **Poor boundaries**
   - Allowing others to take advantage of you or disrespect your limits
   - Struggling to say no and assert your needs
6. **Perfectionism**
   - Setting unrealistically high standards for yourself
7. **Fear of failure**
   - Avoiding new challenges and opportunities due to fear of not succeeding
8. **Overdependence on others**
   - Relying heavily on others for validation and decision-making
9. **Chronic stress and anxiety**
   - Constantly feeling overwhelmed
   - Difficulty relaxing and enjoying the present moment
10. **Difficulty with self-care**
    - Neglecting physical, emotional, and mental health needs
11. **Imposter syndrome**
    - Feeling like a fraud despite evident accomplishments
    - Fear of being exposed as incompetent
12. **Resentment and bitterness**
    - Holding on to grudges and past hurts
13. **Fear of rejection**
    - Avoiding social interactions and opportunities due to fear of being rejected
14. **Inconsistent motivation**
    - A defeated attitude toward tasks before beginning them
    - Struggling to maintain long-term perseverance

This list does not solely apply to a damaged relationship with yourself; these signs can also come from other things such as having ADHD and other psychological and situational factors.

→ WRITE IT DOWN: Are You Your Own Bully?

Reflecting on your relationship with self, I want you to consider if you have been acting like your own best friend or your own biggest bully!

> Write the following questions and answer them in your journal:
> - Is my relationship with self a loving one?
> - Do I actively show myself that I care about myself in the same way I show I care for others?

Now think about some of the negative things you may say to yourself that would get you canceled online if you said them to someone else! Write them in your journal.

Underneath your negative self-talk write the question: Would you sever ties with a friend who repeatedly spoke to you this way?

I know I would have broken up with my negative self because of the things I used to say to myself! Your self-dialogue is not in alignment with the level of kindness you expect from your relationship with others, and you need to hold yourself to the same level of expectations. It's time to break up with the bully and become your own best friend.

→ WRITE IT DOWN: Forgiving Yourself

Before we transform you into your own best friend, you need to forgive yourself for the breakdown of your relationship with self. Answer this: Has a friend or family member ever said something to upset you that you have forgiven and you continued to have a loving relationship with them? We all have! No one is perfect, and sometimes people say things they don't mean and we give them grace in these moments.

In your journal, write a letter of apology to yourself. This is going to push you past your self-hate barrier. It may help to imagine you have said to a best friend the unkind things you say to yourself, and you really want their understanding and forgiveness.

Once you have finished writing your letter, read it back to yourself.

Finish the exercise by writing the words "I forgive you."

The Best-Friend Perspective: Give Yourself Love and Care

Have you ever noticed that when you meet someone like you, you . . . like them? Seeing ourselves in others actually draws us to them. That's because on some level, whether you consciously feel it or not, you do like yourself.

If you could split yourself into two so you had someone to share in your exact interests, talk about exactly what you love to talk about, spend time with them with total comfort in the exact way you like to spend your time, it would be an instant best-friend relationship. You just need to reconnect to yourself and see yourself through a best friend's eyes!

When Being Your Own Best Friend Is Most Important

Becoming emotionally dysregulated is a common occurrence with being ADHD. Feelings come flooding in and our day can quickly veer off course. The emotional fallout we experience after these temporary moments is usually more difficult than the peak of dysregulation.

We tend to beat ourselves up after and punish ourselves in a way we would never treat others. Feelings of frustration, guilt, and shame quickly follow our temporary dysregulated states and can then prolong the experience far past being a moment of emotional flooding.

These instances are where being your own best friend is going to be the most beneficial for you.

Imagine a friend has just become extremely emotionally dysregulated. They expressed how stressed and overwhelmed they felt, then they stormed off and burst into floods of tears. Once you see that the emotional flooding has calmed, you walk over to comfort them. You let them know that they are okay to have felt this way. You listen to them, give them time, and show them empathy, love, and support.

Unless you are a heartless robot, I doubt you would ever walk over to a friend and tell them that they should now be extremely frustrated with themselves, that they should feel guilty for having a flood of emotions, and worst of all, that they should be ashamed!

Becoming Your Own Best Friend

The following questions are going to help you ditch feeling indifferent, ignite self-love, and guide you into the headspace of being your own best friend whenever you need to support yourself.

- How would I comfort a friend right now?
- What would I say to a friend to make them feel better?
- What loving reassurance would I give them?
- What do I think they need to hear from me to help them let go of feelings of frustration, guilt, and shame?

Connect to Your Higher Self

I started developing the "my own best friend" concept years ago when a friend of mine told me to give advice to myself as if I were my own friend. She saw that I gave great advice but didn't apply it to myself. Relatable, right?

As a result, I began to momentarily detach myself from negative situations I was experiencing and imagine a friend asking me for advice about whatever it was I was going through. I didn't realize it at the time, but I was practicing visualization and connecting to my higher self.

After unknowingly doing this for years, I connected with a life coach who took me on a healing journey. She would often refer to "my higher self," and she gave me a visualization practice similar to that of my own, where I imagined myself knocking on my door asking for help, and I welcomed myself in and was there for me.

Your higher self is the version of you that has no ego or worries about your everyday concerns. It is detached from the spikey emotions you feel in the moment and instead embodies wisdom, insight, and awareness to guide you toward the right path. Your higher self has only good intentions. It offers you a sense of inner peace, clarity, and direction.

The best-friend perspective—or higher-self connection—doesn't have to be limited to our negative moments or times of need. We are always in need of that loving connection, especially during moments of achievement and success. You are not only going to be there for yourself when you feel gloomy. You are going to show up for yourself, celebrate yourself, and be your own personal cheerleader!

→ WRITE IT DOWN: Give Yourself Guidance

In your journal, ask a question you would like the answer to around a current issue you are facing. Example: Is this friend good for me or is it time to move on?

Then close your eyes and imagine a version of yourself that has it all figured out. That version of you has a huge smile on their face and an air of peace and confidence. You know that they hold the answer you are looking for. They are without judgment and ego, and they are detached from the emotions that are linked to your situation. All they want is to give you guidance. Ask them your question and see what comes up.

Once you have an answer, write it down as they spoke it to you.

Now look over what advice and guidance you gave yourself. This came from within you. Your emotionally intelligent, ego-free, supportive higher self lives within!

Become Your Own Cheerleader

Years of fearing being too loud and lively for others means you have actively tried to not take up too much space. You tried to avoid hogging a moment or shining too brightly in case it made others reject you. This is about to change. You are allowed to take up space!

A deep way to look at this would be to think about your final day on the planet. Do you think you would ever regret living too largely? Would you regret the moments you shined? Would you regret the occasions you celebrated yourself, the instances you laughed loudly, or the times you got lost in conversations that you are passionate about?

I repeat, *you are allowed to take up space!*

Celebrate Yourself!

Not only are you allowed to be seen and be seen vibrantly, but you are also allowed to celebrate yourself. Having ADHD usually comes with a natural skill of party planning— we're natural event taskmasters, and we use these excitement-driven multitasking skills on all our loved ones. We make sure that others feel special when they have done something wonderful in their life or we feel it is their time to shine on their birthday, anniversary, or even breakup party! You need to do this for yourself too. Don't worry, you can start small.

Entry-Level Cheerleading

Here are three entry-level ways to cheer yourself on:

1. **Give yourself a high five!** It may seem a little goofy, but believe me, in those moments when you have done something you are happy about, there is no better feeling than saying an enthusiastic "Yes!" and high-fiving yourself!
2. **Like your own social media posts.** I like every single one of my posts that I upload on social media. If I didn't like my post, I wouldn't post it, so to physically like it with the button makes sense! Affirming that I like something I shared with the world feels so liberating, and it shows myself an unapologetic level of self-support.
3. **Say out loud, "Well done, me!"** This is self-explanatory. Anything you do—sending an email you were putting off, completing a small task, decorating a room by yourself—tell yourself, "Well done!" Say it as enthusiastically as possible. I usually elongate the *me* of "Well done, me," and I smile as I say it. It feels so rewarding to acknowledge myself in this way.

Intermediate-Level Cheerleading

Once you have practiced and perfected your entry-level cheers, it's time to move on to intermediate level!

1. **Tell someone else, "I am so proud of myself."** Sharing that you are proud of yourself for something you have accomplished is so uplifting. Often the person you share this with will agree with you and share in your moment of pride.
2. **Share your wins with others!** Big or small, if you have done something that feels like a win, tell someone about it and let yourself express the joy that you feel in this moment.
3. **Celebrate yourself.** Acknowledge and reward yourself for even the smallest accomplishments. Keeping a journal of daily victories is a great way to acknowledge your achievements and show yourself how proud you are of what you have done.

Championship-Level Cheerleading

Here are three things you can do to upgrade your cheers:

1. *Really* **celebrate yourself.** In the same way we celebrate others for their accomplishments, we can do this for ourselves. Recently I hit a milestone on social media that I was really proud of, and I immediately bought myself balloons! You can buy yourself a treat, flowers, a dinner out or celebratory takeout—whatever you would want to do for someone else to celebrate them, do it for yourself!

2. **Host a celebration.** We host birthday parties, weddings, baby showers, and so on, so why shouldn't we host celebratory occasions for other achievements and big moments? You better believe that I will be having a book-published party!
3. **Bet on yourself.** Betting on yourself means having the confidence to invest in yourself and your personal growth. Stay committed to your dreams. Trust in yourself to be the one who wins!

Throughout this chapter you may have had some negative self-talk creep into your mind without being consciously aware. Reflect on how you may have been speaking to yourself. I will continue to remind you to be mindful of the thoughts and feelings that you have, because each time you are mindful, you are harnessing the power to actively choose your thoughts instead of slipping into habitual negative self-talk.

Reflect and Act:
Improve Your Relationship with You

Hug yourself every day. The act of self-hugging releases oxytocin, the "feel-good" hormone that helps improve mood and creates a sense of comfort and security. It also reinforces self-love and self-acceptance, making it a simple yet effective tool for self-care.

Give self-encouragement. Encourage yourself just as a best friend with good intentions would. Give yourself a high five, fist-pump the air, bet on yourself to win!

Provide self-care. Now that you are connecting to your higher self and being your own best friend, the more basic self-care practices such as face masks, bubble baths, and cups of hot chocolate are perfect additions to your overall loving relationship with self. Whatever self-care means to you, add more of it into your days.

Strengthen your inner child connection. Do something every day for your inner child. If you are pressed for time, squeeze in singing a song at the top of your lungs if your younger self would have enjoyed that. I fit in little moments of inner child connection by breaking into a skip as I walk my dog. Little me loved skipping! Other inner child activities are doing arts and crafts, dancing however your body wants to, playing games, baking, being active outdoors, or watching favorite childhood movies.

→ WRITE IT DOWN: Be Your Own Best Friend and Cheerleader

Adopting your new best-friend perspective and connecting to your higher self, write down three positive things about what you have learned from this chapter and how you plan to implement having a better relationship with yourself.

Now think about how you are going to guide yourself during difficult times. Consider how you will accept yourself in moments of emotional dysregulation.

Write down the plans you have for showing up for yourself as your biggest cheerleader and supporter.

For many of us, coming back to self and caring for ourselves can really highlight that we have abandoned our own needs. Next you'll learn how to take care of yourself through life-changing reparenting techniques.

The Most Important Things You Need to Know

- The mask we wore so very tightly to conceal all our felt flaws and differences means that we swallowed down every time we felt we didn't do something quite right. Each instance becomes internalized and manifests as a lack of self-belief, self-care, and self-trust.
- The best-friend perspective means treating yourself with the kindness, love, and care that you give to others. It is showing acceptance, forgiveness, and compassion to yourself in times of need and celebrating *you* during moments of accomplishment.
- Your higher self is the version of you that has no ego or worries about your everyday concerns. Your higher self can guide you without feeling the emotions that are attached to negative situations or difficult decisions.
- Cheer yourself on whenever you can! Start with the entry-level cheering and work your way up to becoming your own championship-level cheerleader!

How to Reparent Yourself:
Learning to Love Who You Truly Are

NOW THAT YOU ARE YOUR OWN BEST FRIEND and biggest cheerleader, it's time to uplevel your newfound self-care perspective and fill yourself with unconditional self-love. This is the kind of protective, loving energy you see in healthy parent-child relationships. While not all parent-child relationships are ideal, the general expectation is that parents care for their children with fierce protection, unconditional love, and unwavering support.

This is the energy I want you to direct inward to yourself. For some people, reflecting on parental relationships can stir up uncomfortable emotions, especially if their experience was less than ideal. If this resonates with you, it is even more crucial to embrace the reparenting methods that follow.

What Is Reparenting?

Reparenting is a therapeutic approach first developed in the 1970s that involves giving yourself the care, nurturing, and support that you ideally should have—but may not have—received as a child. The approach focuses on healing inner wounds, building self-love, and developing healthy coping mechanisms by providing yourself with the same kindness and protection that a loving parent would provide.

Unmet ADHD Needs

I assume most readers are adults who grew up when ADHD wasn't widely known or understood. During that time, only a few experts were familiar with it, and they were hard to find. Even then, many experts were still running with the theory that ADHD only affects male children. It's safe to say research was limited, and this likely resulted in you having unmet needs, no matter how wonderful your parents may have been to you.

Five unmet needs ADHDers commonly experienced during their childhood and teenage years include:

1. **Misunderstood behavior:** ADHD symptoms were often misinterpreted as "bad" behavior, laziness, or oversensitivity. These misinterpretations can lead to low self-worth and frustration.
2. **Misdiagnosis or no diagnosis:** Without a proper diagnosis, children don't get the support they need, such as therapy, medication, or educational help. This oversight creates a sense of being misunderstood by those meant to help.
3. **Educational support:** Schools can fail to recognize ADHD, leading to academic struggles and conflict with parents if they don't understand why their child is falling behind. Such misinterpretation can damage self-esteem.
4. **Parental misunderstanding:** Parents lacking full knowledge of ADHD may have felt overwhelmed and frustrated, impacting their ability to be patient and nurturing. This lack of parental support could lead you to suppress and avoid negative emotions.
5. **Social struggles:** Difficulty managing emotions, impulses, and attention can affect social interactions, potentially leading to withdrawal, isolation, or even bullying by peers who misunderstand. Adults may fail to recognize the underlying causes, further complicating the situation, potentially causing loneliness and vulnerability.

Connect to Your Inner Child and Teenager

To adopt a self-loving mindset and foster self-compassion, you need to embody your higher self by connecting to your inner child and teenager. When you are connecting with your younger self and offering them comfort, guidance, and love, you are doing it from a higher-self state!

ADHD 101: ADHD Compassion Is Complicated

Studies show ADHD makes us highly compassionate toward others but less so toward ourselves. ADHD sensitivity makes you more empathetic, deeply experiencing others' emotions and resonating with their feelings. Compassion comes easily because you feel what they feel.

The ADHD expert and psychiatrist Edward Hallowell said in a social media post, "People who have ADHD like me tend to be sensitive–intuitive. We can almost feel what people are feeling before they themselves know what they are feeling. . . We can empathize unbelievably well. We can get into the other person's world and know what they are feeling and thinking."

However, your hardened, self-critical state means you struggle to mirror this compassion back onto yourself. You need a little help doing so. An ADHD study in the *Journal of Clinical Psychology* in 2022 concluded that "self-compassion may be a welcome clinical intervention that could benefit all adults with ADHD." They explained that self-compassion can be cultivated through compassion-focused therapy or daily self-taught practices. This is what you will learn how to do now!

→ DIY Guided Visualization for Your Inner Child

Let's begin with a guided visualization. I often do this with my clients, but you can do a DIY version and bring your inner child's needs to the surface.

- Imagine yourself between the ages of five and ten years old. Using a picture of your younger self works well too! Once you have your younger self as an image in a photo or in your mind, remind yourself that they are you and you are them.
- Take notice of you having the same eyes, the same heart, the same physical mind. Then be mindful of you having the same needs, the same vulnerability, and sensitivities.
- Next you are going to directly ask what unmet needs you have carried through to adulthood. You will talk back and forth with your younger self.

→ WRITE IT DOWN: Six Steps to Connecting with Your Inner Child

A written practice often works even better with your ADHD mind because the motion of writing puts you into a focused flow state.

1. **Begin by writing "You: Hello, little one."** You can change this to say "Hello, little me," "Hello, little [*your name*]," "Hey you"—whatever feels right for you.

2. **Let your younger self reply.** For example:
   Me: Hello, little one
   Little me: Hello!

3. **Explain why you are connecting and what you want to find out from them.** Use your own words but make sure that you directly ask what they need from you to feel loved, safe, and supported. For example:
   Me: I want to make sure you're okay and to see what I can do to make you feel safer, more loved, and better supported. What do you need from me?

4. **Let your younger self respond.** She or he might say things like, "I feel lonely and want to see my friends more." You can probe them for more information.

This practice can be as long or short as you like. When you speak with your inner child, make sure you give reassurance, understanding, and love. I have even apologized to my younger self during these journal practices and asked for forgiveness for not showing up for them/me as they/I needed to.

5 **Bring the conversation to a close by saying "I am here for you. I love you."**

6. **Reflect on what came up.** This should include brainstorming what you can do to meet your unmet needs going forward. Write this down.

You may feel resistance to this practice. I did. But then I reframed it as being an impactful hack that lets you bypass your ego and persona. It allows your vulnerabilities to be heard so that you can take positive action toward taking better care of yourself.

→ FIVE-MINUTE RESET: Stretch and Reset

Reflecting on your past can cause emotions to bubble up. So, let's release some of them with some light movement before we continue.

- Notice each part of your body from your face to your toes. As you do, squeeze each area, focusing on one muscle at a time. When you let go, imagine all tension and built-up emotions being released.
- Next, give yourself a big full-body stretch in whatever way feels best for you.
- If you can, stand up, shake, jump, and shimmy your body to re-regulate your nervous system.
- Take a deep breath in and out, noticing the calmness wash over you.

→ WRITE IT DOWN: How to Reparent Your Inner Teenager

You'll connect with your inner teenager in the same way as your inner child. Look at a photograph of yourself as a teenager and connect with your eyes, noticing they are the same, your heart is the same, and your unmet needs may be the same.

In your journal, begin to write a letter to your teenage self like this:

Dear Teenage [*your name*]

You are writing to your teenage self because they have *big* feelings and would be really excited to receive a letter like this. Instead of asking about unmet needs, give them full validation. Show understanding, reassurance, hope, empathy, compassion, love, and support.

Then tell your teenage self how you'll look out for them. Let them know you can now advocate for yourself as an adult and that you're learning how to feel self-love and be your own best friend and cheerleader!

Here is a short example:

Dear Teenage Claire,

I know how you're feeling. School's tough, your emotions are up and down, and you're confused. But trust me, you're going to be okay—I've got your back! What feels overwhelming now, like being too sensitive, will one day become a trait you cherish. I know it's exhausting, but I'm working on it! I'll make sure you never feel unheard again. I'll give you a confident voice that empowers both you and others. I'll always love and support you.

Love from your grown-up self,
Claire

When you've finished your letter, picture your teenage self being told, "A letter has come for you." You see your name in your own handwriting, open it, and notice it's signed "Love from your grown-up self." Excitement takes over as you find a private spot to read it. Now read the letter back to your teenage self. Let every validating moment sink in. Feel the safety, reassurance, protection, understanding, compassion, and most of all, the love.

Make Connecting with Your Younger Self a Habit

While journal practices are effective, how do you make keeping this connection a habit so that it makes a lasting difference in your life? These activities will keep you in touch with your younger self everyday:

1. **A photo of your younger self:** Place a photo of your younger self where you'll see it daily—on your desk, mirror, or bedside table. I kept mine in my planner. Seeing it reminds you of their unmet needs and motivates you to send love and kind thoughts.
2. **A moment in the mirror:** Look into your eyes and connect with your inner child. Add loving affirmations like, "I am safe," "I am worthy of love," and "I feel joy." Remember, you're speaking to a vulnerable part of yourself that craves loving affection.
3. **Heartbeat connection:** Place your hands on your chest, close your eyes, breathe deeply, and feel your heartbeat. Remind yourself that the little you, with the same heart, is still there. Promise to care for them—always.
4. **Inner-voice connection:** In tough moments, use the written reparenting techniques you've learned but in your mind. Ask yourself if you're okay and see what comes up.
5. **Carry the connection:** Make your younger self your phone background or screensaver. A family photo works if you feel awkward.

I took carrying the connection a step further and had a personalized locket made. On one side is a picture of my seven-year-old self. I first did this on my wedding day because I was so scared that I would ruin the moment when I looked in the mirror in my wedding dress and begin to pick myself apart. But little me didn't deserve that to happen. This was her dream day! She deserved to hear loving things when she looked in the mirror and saw herself as a bride. I have worn an inner-child locket ever since and give it a little squeeze if I need a quick connection.

Establishing Protective Boundaries: You Get to Choose Who Is in Your Life

Think about overprotective helicopter parents who keep their kids wrapped in bubble wrap for safety. While they may go overboard, they're trying to create safe boundaries in what they see as an unsafe world. Their goal is to protect.

As adults, have we been too relaxed with ourselves? Are you letting people in while ignoring warning signs, red flags, and the protective-parent energy that says, "Absolutely *not!*" Setting boundaries is a powerful way to protect yourself.

Boundaries are limits and rules we set to safeguard our well-being and personal space. They ensure we're treated with respect, keep our interactions healthy, and play a crucial role in determining who we allow into our lives and how we maintain existing relationships.

All boundaries are important, but a **self-worth boundary** is a limit we set to protect our sense of value, dignity, and self-respect. It involves recognizing and asserting our worthiness to be treated with kindness, respect, and consideration.

Bluntly speaking, if someone continuously makes you feel like total crap, they are disrespecting your self-worth boundary. In this instance, what would the bubble-wrap parent do? Would they welcome the bully into your home, make them dinner, and let you continue having playdates? Or would they tell you that you don't deserve that?

This is what you can do for yourself now that you have connected with your inner younger you! You've tapped into your protective nature, and while setting boundaries and asserting your self-worth may have been tough before, it won't be a challenge for you moving forward.

Selfishness versus Self Preservation

After lots of me-me-me teachings in this chapter, you may feel a little self-consumed, especially because you are used to caring for everyone but yourself! But rest assured, becoming selfish is highly unlikely for those with ADHD because our heightened empathy naturally fosters a caring nature. Alongside all the entrepreneurial and creative careers that we hurl ourselves into, assuming roles where we care for others is another common path within the ADHD community.

But it's not selfish to look out for yourself too! Taking care of yourself gives you the space to care for others without neglecting your needs in the process. Moreover, being selective about *who* you choose to extend your caring nature toward means you will feel good about doing so.

Surrounding yourself with kind, loving, and supportive people who uplift you rather than bring you down is priority number one when it comes to setting self-worth boundaries! Choose your company wisely and you will create a life bursting with the love, care, and support that lives within you.

In the beginning, making ourselves a priority and setting healthy boundaries can feel strange or even wrong. This makes sense since we're not used to prioritizing our needs over others. However, understanding our self-worth, setting boundaries, prioritizing ourselves, and ending negative relationships are not selfish acts but rather acts of self-preservation.

The Most Important Things You Need to Know

- Reparenting means giving yourself the same kindness and protection that a loving parent would provide to a child.
- No matter if you had a wonderful or crappy childhood, most ADHDers had many important unmet needs because of the lack of research and knowledge about ADHD.
- Daily inner-child/teenager connection is a wonderful way to kick-start acting from your higher self. It increases self-love, self-care, and self-compassion.
- Setting boundaries is an act of knowing your self-worth, self-love, and self-preservation—not selfishness!

Comfort in the Chaos:
Ditching Negative Brain Stimulation

AFTER LEARNING HOW TO BE YOUR OWN BEST FRIEND, how to look after yourself like a doting parent, and who you need to set boundaries with or maybe even ditch, you are going to learn what aspects of yourself also need to be ditched! Sounds harsh, but it's not as harsh as the negative brain stimulation you may have become accustomed to. This chapter is all about becoming self-aware and removing the unconscious bad brain habits that can actively make us feel stressed!

We all know what stress feels like, but did you know that stress is a must-have hormonal response from the body? This response all starts with a part of your brain called the hypothalamus. When you are stressed, the hypothalamus sends signals throughout your nervous system and to your kidneys. In turn, your kidneys release stress hormones, which include adrenaline and cortisol. Why does our body do this? To survive!

We have two survival systems at work: the sympathetic system triggers the fight-or-flight response, preparing the body for action by increasing heart rate and slowing digestion; the parasympathetic system promotes the rest-and-digest response, calming the body and conserving energy after stress. When we perceive danger, cortisol surges and triggers the fight-or-flight response, which can save our lives. It also increases the availability of substances such as glucose and amino acids that repair tissues. You know, in case you were fighting a bear and got injured!

Adrenaline boosts our energy supplies so that we can run faster and farther away from the perceived danger, or fight and defend ourselves. Adrenaline also increases focus so that we can avoid stumbling while defending ourselves, and most impressively it increases muscle strength to ensure we kick their ass! The entire process is quite magical, and its sole purpose is to ensure our safety.

So why does it feel so . . . uncomfortable? Maybe because 99 percent of the time that we feel stressed and the fight-or-flight response kicks in, we aren't in any actual danger. For the modern world we live in, we are pretty safe (for the most part), making this bodily function pretty outdated.

So we get stressed out when we see a social media post while we are safe in our own bed. We enter the fight-or-flight mode when we are late for work and stuck in traffic. We let cortisol surge through us because our house is a mess and a friend is coming over. Our bodies didn't get the memo that we have evolved to the point that not every stressor requires the full-blown fight-or-flight response!

We absolutely need to be able to quickly enter into fight or flight, and we rely on these hormones to help us, but sometimes they cause collateral damage. Noradrenaline is what makes the hormone adrenaline, but if overused, it can:

- **Deplete you of noradrenaline:** This leads to a decrease in focus, low blood pressure, and potential depression and anxiety.

- **Deplete you of dopamine:** This leads to a lack of motivation, lack of pleasure, depression, and fatigue.

- **Inhibit your immune system:** Stress can literally make you sick!

This is general information on stress, but did you know that stress makes ADHD symptoms worse? So why don't we make more effort to de-stress?

Are You Addicted to Stress?

Even with the negatives that stress brings us, it can be extremely addictive. Alongside the fight-or-flight hormones, stress gives us bursts of dopamine, the feel-good chemical. This hormone is very clever because it will get us to repeat behaviors that activate the reward center of our brain to get the burst of dopamine again. You literally seek stress to get the reward!

Not only that, but ADHD means we are very easily bored. Light chitchat and steady days can feel like a total yawn fest. Give us something spicy! With stress pumping so many hormones around the body that all feel intense, we feel incredibly stimulated. Be honest with yourself—are you the drama? Is it you? Consider if you ever seek this sort of brain stimulation. I certainly did!

Hi, I'm Claire, and I'm a Recovering Stress Addict

When I was a child, stressful situations and emotions would make me retreat. I was, just like most children, someone who was on the flight side of fight or flight. However, when I got to my teenage years, a long-term negative relationship that was filled with spiky cortisol-pumping moments taught my brain that stress was stimulating and came with a burst of dopamine.

It was the months leading up to my ADHD diagnosis that really revealed this to me. I had been self-medicating through smoking and vaping on and off for years. I decided I wanted to quit for good, but my body missed all that extra dopamine.

So what did I do? I caused absolute f*cking chaos! I needed dopamine and stimulation from wherever I could find it, and my clever little dopamine-chasing brain had learned that stress provides exactly that. My relationship with my now husband went to a temporary ruin, and when I was sitting alone wondering what on earth was happening to me, I reflected hard.

I realized: This is me. I am causing chaos.

The realization that I was the source of the chaos in my life sent me on a total deep dive into the world of stress. I discovered that we can not only seek stress for the stimulation and dopamine but chaos can feel comforting to us.

Chaos can be comforting if you've had a chaotic upbringing or relationships because it's familiar and predictable in its unpredictability. When chaos is a constant presence in your early life, it can become your "normal." You might find stability or a strange sense of control in knowing how to navigate turbulent situations. In contrast, calm and stable environments can feel unfamiliar and unsettling, leading to discomfort or anxiety. Essentially chaos becomes a comfort zone because it's what you're accustomed to.

This information made me reflect on my upbringing, which I had always painted as an idyllic picturesque setting with rainbows and unicorns. But the reality of my upbringing is, although I adore my parents, and they have given me an endless supply of happy memories, they were also pretty damn chaotic!

The dining room often served as a hub for new business ventures, which would fill the house with excitement and stress. Our house was always full, whether it was friends, relatives, or builders for whatever work was currently being done. Having only the five of us was a rarity. Even planning a family vacation was both exciting and exhausting, filled with loud and lengthy phone calls and endless decision-making marathons. We each had our own hobbies, a pet for every person, and *big* emotions about everything. A family crisis could come from a minor inconvenience. It was a whirlwind—busy, fast-paced, and always unpredictable.

Upon reflection as a now calm and in-control-of-my-emotions adult (for the most part), I can see that little things were often turned into extra-big deals, or at least it felt that way to me as a child. I can see now that this was probably due to having an undiagnosed neurodivergent parent—my dad—who would become overwhelmed and emotionally dysregulated.

This information also made me reflect on what my first romantic relationship taught my brain. With that, I took my sorry ass back to my husband and begged for his forgiveness and support while I navigated getting an ADHD diagnosis.

ADHD 101: Do You Seek Dopamine from Stress and Chaos?

Now it's your turn. Take a moment to reflect on your life. Have your experiences taught your brain to seek stress and boost yourself up with dopamine?

Do you . . .
- Wait until the very last minute to submit work, forms, and so forth?
- Point out problems with work, your environment, people?
- Feel like you thrive in high-pressure situations?
- Disrupt calm environments?
- Cause unnecessary arguments?
- Create a sense of urgency to feel motivated?
- React negatively to small inconveniences?
- Enjoy the excitement of unpredictability and fast-paced situations?
- Struggle to relax or enjoy downtime without feeling bored?
- Seek out stumbling blocks when things are going smoothly?

Negative Self-Boosting

As a result of being unaware of this type of brain stimulation-seeking, we can normalize giving ourselves boosts negatively. I call this "negative self-boosting," and it actually came to me when I was just twenty-one years old and I had the pleasure of working alongside someone who did this constantly. They would drag everyone down around them to lift themselves up.

There are a few reasons why we might negative self-boost. One is very ego led. We can put someone down to feel better about ourselves. Imagine placing your hands on someone's shoulders and lifting yourself up. The person would be pushed down a little as you rise. The problem with this is, you can't stay there all day. As you release your hands from their shoulders, you stumble farther down than you were before. Ouch!

Bottom line: when we try to increase our sense of self-worth by putting someone down, we inevitably feel worse for doing it. It is a vicious cycle that teaches your brain that you can get a quick hit of dopamine with unkindness and judgment, so you repeat the process to get the short-lived brain reward and ultimately become the office asshole. You can also negative self-boost through any kind of negative interaction. When I think about the Karens of the world, I always wonder what sort of chaos they have experienced in their lives to now seek stress in every situation. Whether it's shouting at a waiter, demanding a refund for the dress they have worn and decided they no longer like, or loudly saying "*Shhh!!*" to a child giggling in the movie theater, they seem to grab every opportunity to feel that comforting chaos, the stimulating stress, and sudden dopamine boost!

Then there's the negative self-boosting I still have to keep in check: productivity stress. This is when stress-seeking disguises itself as something beneficial. We dress up overcommitting as being a boss, overworking as being a go-getter, and overwhelming ourselves with ten people's workload as being a multitasking superhuman. But it's all make-believe. We are negative self-boosting via our workload!

Yes, it's in our ADHD nature to want to explore a million things, but do you ever catch yourself actively taking on more even though you outright *know* you are far too stressed to do so? This could be you creating a chaotic lifestyle that feels comforting to you and spices up your life to a point of you being in a constant state of fight or flight.

ADHD: Keeping It Simple

Are You Negative Self-Boosting?

Do you . . .

- Gossip about and act unkind toward others to make yourself feel better?
- Seek drama or create conflict to feel a rush of excitement?
- Show anger toward someone for a human error or simple mistake?
- Make a big deal out of small situations, such as someone forgetting something?
- Remind people of their imperfections or past mistakes?
- Engage in excessive criticism, overanalyze other people's behavior, or judge others?
- Manipulate situations or people to feel a sense of control?
- Spread misinformation or fabricate the truth to feel important and better than others?
- Knowingly overcommit, overwork, or overwhelm yourself with too much to do?
- Have an overflowing schedule that is humanly impossible to commit to?
- Write a years' worth of to-dos for you to complete in a day? (Disclaimer: This trait can also be due to time blindness.)

Positive Self-Boosting: Choose Your Stressor

Before I share my top three self-boosting switches for healthier brain stimulation and more dopamine, keep this in mind: both negative and positive self-boosting can feel stressful. The way you've been seeking stimulation may be causing prolonged stress on your body, worsening your ADHD symptoms over time. While these positive switches might feel just as difficult at first, the discomfort is temporary and doesn't come with the lasting negative effects of negative self-boosting. Instead, they bring long-term benefits to your brain, body, and ADHD. So, while both options can feel challenging, it's up to you to choose your hard.

Here are my top three favorite self-boosting practices. They all boost the dopamine in your brain in a much healthier way.

Exercise

Cortisol is released during exercise, which is a normal and healthy response, making exercise the perfect switch from negative to positive self-boosting. Regular exercise improves the body's ability to manage stress and regulate cortisol levels more effectively. Although cortisol levels spike (just as you like them to) during activity, exercise helps maintain healthy cortisol rhythms overall.

My go-to workout is running, not because I'm great at it but because it stimulates my brain just right. The goal is to switch your stressors to something positive. For me, running is a stressor before I even begin, sparking an internal conflict that satisfies my brain's craving for stimulating struggle. It triggers a healthy amount of cortisol and releases happy hormones. I find outdoor running far more stimulating than exercising indoors. As I run, I process everything around me quickly, which suits my ADHD brain perfectly. It's important to explore different activities and find what works best for you.

Cold-Water Therapy

If you immediately said "Hell no," then consider that it might be *exactly* what you need. If you're addicted to stress, what better way to overcome it than to plunge yourself into a body of water that puts your body into a state of heightened alertness and stimulation?

To begin, you can do a cold-water face plunge in the sink or bowl with or without ice for one to three minutes, which has many of the same benefits as submerging your entire body. Switching your shower from hot to cold at the end for a few minutes is also a good introduction to cold-water therapy. I prefer the full plunge! I got an outdoor plunge tub that wasn't expensive. I then got my husband to build it a wooden home. It looks like a big beehive now! But if you want to go for it, you can get a refrigerated plunge tub installed. For now, I will stick to my DIY beehive and rubber-ducky thermometer.

Cold-water exposure actually activates the sympathetic nervous system, triggering the fight-or-flight response. But overtime, repeated exposure helps regulate the body's stress response, leading to *reduced* levels of stress hormones, such as cortisol. Hell yes to that!

Mood Music

Listening to music is a game changer, and I don't mean the clinky, calming kind. That is great if you're meditating and want to nurture a state of calmness and relaxation, but that's not really the point of this strategy.

Depending on your mood, you can listen to:

Rage music: Listening to songs that resonate with your emotions provides a healthy outlet for expressing and processing feelings of anger, sadness, and frustration.
Focus music: I made the mistake of playing calming music when I worked and realized it made me feel sleepy and lose focus. Then off I would go on a journey away from work to find something more stimulating. But as soon as I switched to "upbeat focus music," I now speed through work.
Positive music: This may sound a little broad, but what I mean is music that doesn't unknowingly seep negativity into your mind. My morning playlist not only stimulates my brain but gets me singing positive affirmations all day long. "I am worthy!" is a welcomed brain worm from one affirmation artist. Another really uplifting one that I sing all the time is "I'm Amazing" by Deraj Global. Simply put, be mindful of what you stream into your mind and play as much uplifting, happy, and positive music as possible.

I know these switches require effort, but so does seeking negative stress. The amount of energy you may currently use to do this is probably completely exhausting. So, choose your hard. I will give you a full dopamine menu in chapter 13. The dopamine menu items solely focus on increasing dopamine, so these will be a little easier for you to adopt into your life.

Your Brain Needs Boredom

As modern humans, we are all overstimulated and super busy. We fill any free time we do have with phone scrolling, messaging, and Netflix bingeing. Has anyone allowed themselves to stop for long enough to consider what effects this has on our brain?

We are supposed to let our brain rest, just like any other part of our body. This frees up our brain to go off on its own unique thinking journey without outside influences. Consider when you were little and would get bored. You would find something fun to do—play make-believe, get creative with art, invent games, and make up songs!

The adult brain isn't any different, but instead of playing make-believe and inventing games, we can let our mind wander, daydream, or think spontaneously. Things like painting freely without a plan of the picture, crocheting, and walking a familiar route are among the best activities to let your mind be completely free. This is your brain in the default-mode network, and it's essential for your brain health.

Begin to Ditch Negative Brain Stimulation

You're on the brink of delving into chapters that offer transformative tools to help you manage what once seemed unmanageable: your emotions, increasing dopamine, managing relationships, task management, and so on. But here are some things you can do right now to begin to feel better.

Digital Overload

Our brains aren't exactly made for the digital clutter we have created in the world. How much screen time do you log? How many open internet tabs do you have? Emails? Notifications? All of these can trigger overstimulation and stress.

Some quick solutions are to turn off the notifications on social apps, hit delete on any unopened email that is over twelve months old (I know you're hoarding tens of thousands of emails!), and use a digital project organizer such as Trello to transfer URLs relating to whatever you are planning and working on so that you can finally *close the goddamn tab!*

Negative News

Limit exposure to negative news stories or media content that can evoke fear, anxiety, and stress. Instead, focus on consuming uplifting and informative content that promotes positivity and well-being. For anyone with ADHD, I would like to impose a ban on starting your day by watching the news. Switch to the happy mood music instead.

Space and Color Clutter

Clutter adds extra stimulation to our brain, constantly signaling that "the work isn't done," which causes cognitive overload. This can lead to a reduced working memory, inhibit creativity and problem-solving, cause a sense of overwhelm and urgency, and boost stress levels and anxiety. Even the colors we choose in our environments can add to becoming overstimulated. For example, red and yellow are extremely stimulating colors. I may have a fifty-shades-of-beige bedroom, but I am one calm little cucumber when I'm in it.

Heavy Language

It is time to ditch the heavy "I have to," "I need to," "I must do" language you are so used to and switch it to things like "I want to," "I'd like to," "I get to." These swaps reduce the pressure and stress associated with urgent-sounding heavy language and puts the emphasis on your choice and desire to achieve. Do you motivate yourself using stressful and pressurized language?

The Most Important Things You Need to Know

- Our body enters the fight-or-flight response to protect us from danger.
- Being stressed too often can deplete our body of noradrenaline and dopamine, which causes decreased focus, low blood pressure, fatigue, lack of motivation and pleasure, increased risk of depression, and anxiety; it also inhibits our immune system.
- Stress can become addictive because of how stimulating it is and the short-lived dopamine reward it triggers.
- Chaos can feel comforting if you are used to experiencing a chaotic environment.
- Switch from negative to positive self-boosting with exercise, cold-water therapy, and mood music.
- Ditch negative brain stimulation and let your brain be bored by entering into the default-mode network.

Emotional Dysregulation:
Understanding Your Ups and Downs

ADHD IS COMMONLY THOUGHT TO BE something that makes a person hyperactive in mind and body, but emotions are a big part of what we struggle with too. Emotional dysregulation is often a leading ADHD symptom for many yet is often completely overlooked.

In fact, the American Psychiatric Association included emotional dysregulation in the official diagnostic descriptions of ADHD in earlier versions of the *Diagnostic and Statistical Manual of Mental Disorders* in the 1970s, but later removed it. Wow!

However, many ADHD adults consider emotional dysregulation to be a part of their experience, making professionals and researchers think it should be reinstated in the official list of symptoms. I do too!

It's easy to feel alone when you have a mental health issue or disorder. So, I want to stress to you that your heightened emotions are an extremely common symptom of ADHD. In fact, a recent study, titled "Emotion Dysregulation in Attention Deficit Hyperactivity Disorder," published in the *American Journal of Psychiatry*, showed that up to 73 percent of the 1,490 participants displayed emotional dysregulation as a symptom of ADHD. *Seventy-three percent is a majority!*

What Is Emotional Dysregulation and Do You Experience It?

Emotional dysregulation describes the difficulty some people have with managing their emotions. Emotions can often feel out of your control, as if they are "taking over" your rational thoughts and neutral state.

Emotional dysregulation can look and feel like:

- Intense feelings
- Sudden changes in emotions
- Quickly becoming overwhelmed
- Spiraling into sadness, anger, excitement, etc.
- Having a low frustration tolerance
- Feeling a sense of urgency and becoming quickly impatient
- Impulsiveness and excitability
- Loss of calm, rational, and critical thinking

People with inattentive and combined types of ADHD can experience this dysregulation internally with no "external explosion" of emotions, because they may struggle to recognize or express feelings and internalize them as anxiety without the visible outbursts of overwhelm.

How Do Emotions Become Dysregulated?

An emotion becomes dysregulated when a single negative emotion triggers multilayered thoughts, which then create more emotions that are all heightened.

That sucks.	That REALLY sucks!	MY LIFE SUCKS!!!!
Something upsets you	**Emotional flooding happens**	**Logic leaves**

As you can see in the graphic, we can go from having a very typical human experience, such as forgetting to take our lunch to work and casually thinking, "That sucks," to then being flooded with heightened feeling—"That *really* sucks!"—due to additional negative thoughts and feelings like "I always forget everything! Why do I always do this?!" This then leads to the irrational conclusion that "*My life sucks!*" because logic has left the building. At this point, we are totally owned by our emotions and become dysregulated.

The initial negative emotion isn't always from a negative situation we are currently experiencing. It can be a negative thought about anything—past, present, future, or even imagined! This is why our thoughts are extremely important.

During emotional flooding, all our thoughts can feel very loud and overcrowded, and this often results in overwhelming feelings and irrational thoughts that don't seem to marry with the situation that caused us to have the initial singular negative emotion.

It's like "emotional spamming" that causes a "brain error," similar to a computer trying to manage too many messages at once, causing it to malfunction!

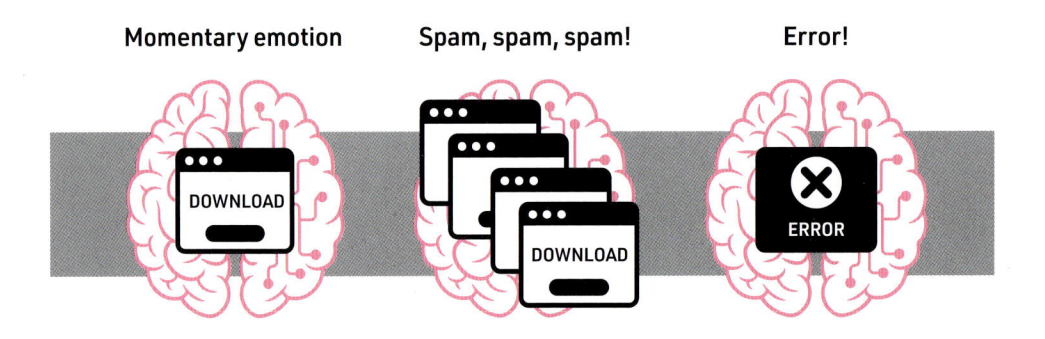

You can "download" a single momentary emotion, then you are suddenly "spammed" by a bunch of unwanted downloads. The spamming is the emotional flooding, and the "error" message is the difficulty in processing all the additional pop-ups (your thoughts and feelings).

Unfortunately we can't just click the X on the pop-up message. We need to reboot the computer, and I will show you exactly how in the next chapter. First, we need to have a full understanding of what emotional dysregulation is and look at preventative measures.

ADHD 101: Why Does the ADHD Community Experience Emotional Dysregulation?

Research published in the *Journal of Affective Disorders* in 2022 studied the relationship between emotional control, cognitive reappraisal, and expressive suppression in ADHDers. Here's your ADHD-friendly summary:

1. Less "Cognitive Reappraisal": Cognitive reappraisal is the ability to change your emotional response to an experience by *choosing* your thoughts and perspective. For example, you see canceled plans as a chance to relax instead of being upset. Adults with ADHD were found to use cognitive reappraisal less frequently, contributing to emotional dysregulation. This is why the reframing techniques you have learned from this book are so important.

2. More "Expressive Suppression": Expressive suppression is when you try to hide facial expressions that match your emotional experience (masking). When you hide or suppress your emotions, it affects the connectivity between two parts of your brain: the amygdala (processes emotions) and the prefrontal cortex (helps control emotions). This weakened connection makes it harder for you to control your emotions.

To bask in your brilliance, here is the clever formula conclusion found in the research paper that you now fully understand without needing to decode anything:

$$\uparrow ES \rightarrow \downarrow FCs \text{ [amygR-PFC]} \rightarrow \downarrow EC$$

Smug faces are welcome.

→ WRITE IT DOWN: What Does Emotional Dysregulation Look and Feel Like to You?

To take control and manage your emotions, you need to know exactly how emotional dysregulation works in your mind and body.

Part 1: Identify Your Emotions

1. **What is the *leading* emotion you feel the most when you become dysregulated?** This can be different for everyone. Some describe it as a feeling of sudden overwhelm, stress or even anger, confusion, frustration, anxiety, defeat, and so on. What do you feel? The goal is for you to be able to pinpoint what emotions trigger dysregulation for you and eventually to be able to prevent them by recognizing the warning signs.
2. **What emotion(s) do you feel the most after it passes?** Think about the feelings you experience once the heightened emotions subside and you have clearer thoughts. It's normal to experience shame, guilt, sadness, exhaustion, and so on. What do you feel?

When you look at the emotions you begin and end with, you start to build a full picture of your emotional dysregulation. Emotional dysregulation often happens because we're not fully aware of how our feelings feel to us. If we recognize the early signs of our negative emotions, we can take steps to prevent them from escalating into emotional flooding.

Think of a time you ignored feeling stressed and carried on with your day. Then a minor stressor tipped you into emotional dysregulation, all because you didn't address the initial singular emotion you felt hours earlier.

Part 2: How My Feelings Feel

Now answer the following questions for each emotion you wrote down:

1. Where do you feel each emotion physically in your body?
2. Does the emotion have movement or is it still?
3. Does it have a temperature (hot/cold)?
4. Does the feeling have a color when you think about it?
5. Does it appear as a shape in your body when you imagine it?

This will help you distinguish between the different emotions that you feel.

Part 3: Tell Someone Else How You Feel

Describe what emotional dysregulation feels like to you as if you are telling someone else about it so they *fully* understand what you experience. What you are really doing here is giving yourself the knowledge to be able to recognize emotional dysregulation within yourself, which will help you take control when you next notice you are starting to feel this way.

How Has Emotional Dysregulation Impacted You?

When we fail to recognize our initial emotion and intervene to avoid becoming emotionally dysregulated, we often self-soothe in unhealthy ways. Try not to give yourself a hard time about this. It's logical to do illogical things when we feel dysregulated.

Common unhealthy coping mechanisms include:

- Impulsive buying
- Prolonged isolation
- Self-hate or self-harm
- Negative self-talk
- Emotional or binge eating
- Smoking or vaping
- Drinking or taking drugs
- Impulsive decision-making
- Cutting off family members and friends
- Breaking up with partners
- Quitting jobs
- Quitting hobbies
- Overworking or being consumed by work
- Dissociating
- Excessive sleeping
- Avoiding responsibilities
- Engaging in risky behaviors
- Excessive TV or gaming
- Excessive social media consumption

To keep it real and help you avoid unnecessary shameful feelings you may have, I have personally coped by using all these mechanisms at one time or another. You are not alone in this, and I am proud of you for attempting to make yourself feel better somehow, even if the way you did wasn't ideal. Most importantly, you're going to learn to cope in healthier ways. If I can do it, you can too.

Unhealthy coping mechanisms act as temporary quick fixes. It's like you've clicked to close the spam pop-ups, but the issue in the hard drive is still there. In fact, unhealthy coping mechanisms often cause *more* negative emotions, such as guilt, shame, embarrassment, and so on.

Understanding the broader impact of emotional dysregulation is crucial as it can profoundly affect your nervous system, mental and physical health, and overall quality of your life. I've just come to terms with its affect on my nervous system and healed myself. Here's what I learned: *Emotional dysregulation causes a dysregulated nervous system, which causes chaos in your life!*

How Dysregulation Strains Your Nervous System

When you frequently become emotionally dysregulated, it places a constant strain on your nervous system because the body's natural stress response is being repeatedly activated. As you learned in the previous chapter, stress triggers your body to pump out the hormones cortisol and adrenaline, which, if released too often, can cause a depletion of noradrenaline leading to depression, anxiety, fatigue, dopamine depletion, and ill health! So, the next time you're tempted to push through negative emotions and become emotionally flooded, remember that your brain and body need to release and regulate.

ADHD 101: Dysregulation

Emotional Dysregulation versus Dysregulated Nervous System

Emotional dysregulation means you have difficulty managing your emotions and responding in a typical or healthy way. It involves struggles with recognizing, understanding, and expressing feelings appropriately.

In contrast, a dysregulated nervous system occurs when the body's stress response malfunctions, often due to prolonged or chronic stress or trauma. This can result in heightened alertness, disrupted sleep and digestion, and . . . emotional dysregulation!

So what came first—the stress causing the challenges in regulating your emotions or the emotional dysregulation causing the stress? Who knows. Let's not focus on the chicken-or-egg scenario.

Do You Need to Regulate Your Nervous System?

Part of regulating your nervous system is catching yourself in those moments of heightened stress and actively doing something to calm yourself down. For a long time I didn't realize I was living with a dysregulated nervous system. I had become so used to the bubbly feeling of anxiety in my chest and the stressful pressure in my head that would keep me in a frantic go-go-go mode!

If you haven't already included stress on your "How My Feelings Feel" list, expand on that now and figure out *exactly* what the fight-or-flight response feels like to you. Also ask yourself, "How often am I in a state of heightened stress? And how often is my body in the fight-or-flight response mode?"

Here are ten signs that you have a dysregulated nervous system:

1. Heightened stress levels
2. Sleep disturbances
3. Digestive issues
4. Emotional instability
5. Fatigue
6. Difficulty focusing
7. Physical tension
8. Hypervigilance
9. Reduced immune function
10. Changes in appetite

Five Uncommon but Effective Ways to Regulate Your Nervous System

1. Release Unhealed Emotional Wounds

Chronic and prolonged stress can be a result of trauma, big or small. If a past situation hasn't been resolved and released, it lives in your body. This is why in the previous chapters I have been asking you to reflect on your past. To continue this work, go back to those practices for other unhealed emotional wounds.

2. Shift Your Perspective and Choose Your Thoughts

With all the reframing practices and perspective shifts you have done, you are primed to become less and less stressed. Remember, your ADHD means you naturally engage less frequently in cognitive reappraisal (the ability to change your emotional response to an experience by choosing your thoughts and perspective). This means you need to be very mindful about doing this.

You could practice now by reframing this scenario in your journal:

You forgot to set an alarm and missed the gym class you planned to go to.

Remember to *choose* calm and kind thoughts and reframe the situation by seeking the positive out.

3. Ground Yourself

The earth is electrically conductive and carries a negative charge. Direct contact with the earth evens out the positive charge that builds up in our bodies from things like our phones, TVs, computers, and so on. Grounding neutralizes the internal bioelectrical environment, which can have major benefits such as reducing fatigue, pain, blood pressure, and anxiety; and improving mood, sleep, depression symptoms, and heart health.

When you feel overwhelmed, head outside, kick off your shoes, and ground yourself for five or more minutes. Make sure to leave your phone and smartwatch inside. For an extra-calming effect, take deep breaths in and out and repeat soothing affirmations to yourself, such as "I am safe, calm, and in control."

4. Try Naturopathic Remedies

To regulate my nervous system, I've tried various natural remedies, such as lion's mane, along with stress-reducing, ADHD-supporting vitamins and nutrients such as B vitamins and magnesium. I've found that Mother Nature offers incredible support for our well-being.

Most recently I have been taking the herb rhodiola, which has been successfully trialed to improve symptoms of chronic stress and burnout. Please do your own research here and always speak to your doctor before taking a new supplement, but this one has worked well for me and the stressful state I was in!

5. Cold-Water Therapy

As I said in the previous chapter, cold-water exposure activates the sympathetic nervous system, triggering the fight-or-flight response. Over time, repeated exposure helps regulate the body's stress response, leading to *reduced* levels of stress hormones such as cortisol. Three, two, one—plunge!

Five More Commonly Heard of Ways to Regulate Your Nervous System

1. Exercise!
2. Breath work
3. Adequate sleep
4. Professional support
5. Emotional regulation techniques

Identifying my emotional dysregulation as one of my main life disruptors was the *exact* thing that transformed my life because I could finally do something about it—get emotionally regulated! You can too. Let's step into your regulated future . . .

The Most Important Things You Need to Know

- Seventy-three percent of those with ADHD display emotional dysregulation as an ADHD symptom.
- In emotional dysregulation, a single negative emotion triggers multiple layers of thought, which then create more emotions that are all heightened, causing emotional flooding.
- Being able to pinpoint what emotions trigger dysregulation for you can help you prevent these moments by recognizing the warning signs of becoming dysregulated.
- When we fail to recognize our initial emotion and intervene to avoid becoming emotionally dysregulated, we can find ourselves self-soothing using unhealthy coping mechanisms.
- Emotional dysregulation causes a dysregulated nervous system, and a dysregulated nervous system causes chaos in your life!

Emotional Regulation:
The Four-Step Self-Soothing System

IN THIS CHAPTER YOU'LL LEARN how to establish an effective four-step self-soothing system to bring your emotions back into balance. Emotions rule our lives, so you *need* to take control if you want to achieve your ADHD reset.

Take a moment to reflect on the ways you've coped when you're emotionally dysregulated. In the previous chapter, I shared a list of common ways of coping, but it's time to get specific.

→ WRITE IT DOWN: How Have You Been Coping?

What do you do when you feel dysregulated? Write down five to ten go-to coping mechanisms, such as:

1. Napping during the day : (
2. Isolating and not talking to people
3. Eating junk food to feel good
4. Talking to my friends and family on the phone
5. Vaping *a lot*!
6. Listening to calming music

Now look over your list and cross out unhealthy ways of coping that are short-lived or that make you feel worse. Then highlight what you are left with (if any). For example:

1. ~~Napping during the day :(~~
2. ~~Isolating and not talking to people~~
3. ~~Eating junk food to feel good~~
4. Talking to friends and family on the phone
5. ~~Vaping a lot!~~
6. Listening to calming music

Doing this gives you an overview of your current coping mechanisms and makes clear which ones you need to ditch or keep.

What Triggers You to Become Emotionally Dysregulated?

Later in this chapter you'll learn specific ways to self-regulate, but first let's take a closer look at why you become emotionally dysregulated in the first place.

In the previous chapter, you learned the science behind emotional dysregulation and that, as an ADHDer, you're prone to becoming emotionally dysregulated. In this chapter, we'll identify which specific triggers cause this for you.

Understanding your triggers and stressors will help you navigate life more easily because you'll be better prepared, more mindful, and more self-aware.

Understanding the Difference Between Stressors and Triggers

Understanding the difference between stressors and triggers is crucial as they both impact our emotions but operate differently. Recognizing the difference can help us manage them more effectively in daily life.

Stressor: Any external or internal stimulus that causes stress. It can be an event, situation, task, or environment that puts pressure on you and causes stress to increase. Examples include deadlines at work, financial problems, noisy environments, or lack of sleep.

Trigger: A specific cue that provokes an *immediate* emotional response, such as an unexpected accident, having an invite rejected, or witnessing an injustice.

A stressor increases overall stress. A trigger (in this context) causes immediate emotional dysregulation. This is an important distinction.

For instance, one of my stressors is being on time for something. A trigger as I'm getting ready could be an item of clothing *unexpectedly* needing to be ironed or dropping a huge blob of foundation on my top.

Because I have become aware of my stressors and triggers, I've made adjustments. I give myself more time than the average person would need. I have spoken with my husband, and he takes over additional responsibilities when I need to get somewhere, such as feeding our dog before we leave. Most importantly, I remain mindful that I am in control of my thoughts and affirm to myself that I am in control and calm throughout! Remember, the study in the previous chapter showed that ADHDers struggle with cognitive reappraisal, i.e., deciding to change your emotional response to situations. Becoming aware of what situations act as stressors (being ready on time) prepares you to react differently if a trigger (dropping makeup on my top) happens during the stressor. Having awareness of your stressors helps you effectively adjust your emotional response prior to potential triggers.

Self-awareness is powerful! Let's do a few journal practices to reveal what your triggers and stressors are!

→ WRITE IT DOWN: What's the Cause?

1. What situations usually result in you feeling *dysregulated*?

I listed:

- Getting ready for a social event
- Packing an overnight bag or suitcase to travel with
- Cooking dinner with lots of different foods that all need different cooking times
- Talking about topics that involve lots of numbers, such as finance
- Having too much to do in one day

2. Are there any themes to when you feel *dysregulated*?

Review all the things you have listed and see if there are any common denominators. Are there any links? For example, when I reviewed my list, I realized that they are all time-bound or number-related stressors!

3. What daily things affect you negatively that don't seem to negatively impact others?

Generating this list will help you become mindful of what unrealistic neurotypical expectations you put on yourself. We live in a neurotypical world, and it can be difficult to manage with our neurodivergent brain! Viewing it this way and writing down the things that impact you should lead to more self-kindness instead of negative self-talk. Some example answers are:

- Getting to work on time
- Cooking dinner
- Noisy environments
- Large crowds of people

All these things are part of life but are *very* common stressors for people with ADHD.

4. What causes you *stress* on a daily basis?

This list will reveal your most obvious stressors and the areas of your life you need to be mindful of that can cause dysregulation. Common stressors for those with ADHD are:

- Traffic jams
- Work deadlines
- House chores, like washing pots or laundry

5. Make a list of things that have happened that *triggered* you into immediate emotional dysregulation.

Reviewing these moments often highlights that you were already within one of your stressor situations. Here are some of my triggers:

- Not being able to find something as I am about to leave the house
- Someone speaking to me rudely
- Being misunderstood and feeling judged
- Breaking something
- Receiving unexpected emails that need urgent responses/action

The Five Control Questions to Ask Yourself

When a task feels like a stressor that could increase the risk of emotional dysregulation, it is extremely helpful to be mindful of the reason why. The *why* holds the power here!

For example, packing a suitcase to travel is a stressor of mine. *Why* is this? Because it's time bound; because I am relying on my memory and don't want to forget anything important. This is what makes this particular task a stressor for me and has led to emotional dysregulation many times in my life! Once you know the why, you can better navigate how to handle a task and avoid becoming dysregulated.

For example, I now pack days in advance, whereas I used to be a last-minute Larry with this! I also make a digital checklist for things I need to get, things I need to pack, *and* things I need to use the morning of but still need to pack on the day of traveling! This was all implemented because I understood the "why" of my stressor.

Reflect and Act:
Reducing Stress Is Your New Mission

The Stress and Emotional Dysregulation Negative Feedback Loop

When you experience stress, you experience emotional dysregulation more frequently. The difficulty in managing your emotions during dysregulation then causes additional stress.

This negative feedback loop perpetuates itself, with each component feeding into the other, and makes it challenging to break free from the ongoing stress and emotional turmoil.

While this chapter's main focus is to take control and reduce moments of emotional dysregulation, I need to stress to you that reducing stress is also a must-do mission.

In the exact same way that stress causes emotional dysregulation, which causes stress that causes emotional dysregulation . . . we can create a similar loop with calmness and control.

Control emotional dysregulation and you reduce stress, which then reduces moments of dysregulation and so on!

Repeat after me: Stress-reducing mission ACCEPTED!

Make a note of the five control questions to ask yourself when a task or situation feels like a stressor:

1. Why does this feel stressful to me?
2. Have I done this or something similar successfully before?
3. Is the task achievable?
4. What parts of the task do I anticipate I'll struggle with?
5. What can I do to make it easier for myself?

I've used these questions a lot! Now that I have used this inquisitive method for so many different things, I use them less and less. I see the "why" in stressors pretty much automatically and make adjustments to make whatever it is as easy and calm as possible for myself.

Sometimes making a task easier requires you to do some preparation before said stressor task, such as writing a detailed and time-ordered travel list days in advance! But it's worth it. I actually enjoy packing now and can finally get excited for my travels instead of being a puddle of crying stress on the floor of my bedroom. True story.

When to Press Pause

Remind yourself of the emotional dysregulation journey your brain goes on with this repeated graphic of emotional dysregulation.

A *single negative emotion* triggers *multilayered thoughts*, which then create *more emotions*, which are all *heightened*.

| That sucks. | That REALLY sucks! | MY LIFE SUCKS!!!! |
| Something upsets you | Emotional flooding happens | Logic leaves |

We want to get to a place where we can press pause during this pattern—ideally in stage one, during the momentary single negative emotion (when something upsets you). But it can often creep up fast, so the true goal is to never enter the point of dysregulation where logic leaves and you are led fully by emotions.

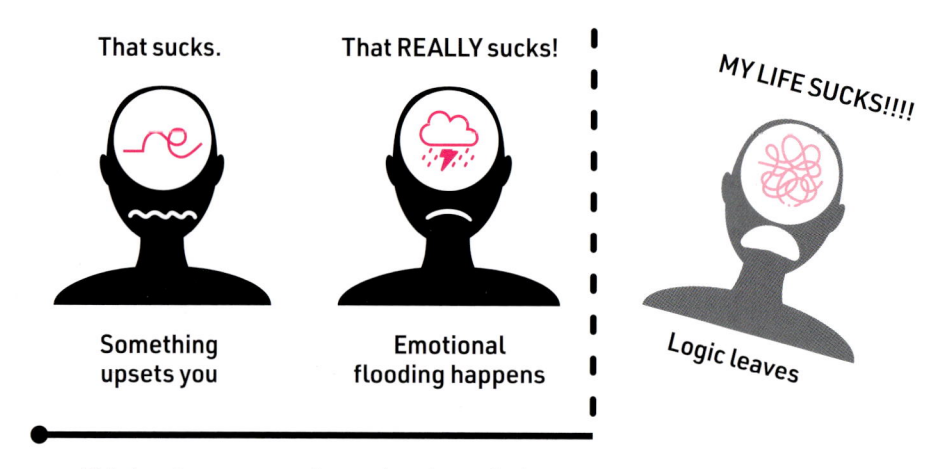

That sucks. | **That REALLY sucks!** | **MY LIFE SUCKS!!!!**

Something upsets you | **Emotional flooding happens** | **Logic leaves**

This is where we need *emotional regulation*.

The aim here is not to shun your emotions away or mask emotional dysregulation but to recognize your emotions in the moment, understand them, identify them as they come up, and regulate them, so you can better avoid that last stage—when logic leaves and you attempt to regulate in unhealthy ways. To achieve this, you need to intervene and cut off that last stage. Goodbye, irrational life-sucking thoughts!

The Four-Step Self-Soothing System

Hopefully by now you've become more aware of why you become dysregulated by stress and specific triggers. Unfortunately you *will* feel that rush of negative emotions again at some point, so you *need* to be fully prepared to take control! I'll show you how.

Step 1: Noticing *What* You Feel and *How* It Feels

Most of us ignore how we feel, which causes feelings to run wild and makes them harder to rein in. You have learned what emotional dysregulation feels like, but this practice should help you identify your emotions in the moment.

For each of the following grouped words, I want you to read them, then close your eyes and say them in your mind again. Speak them out loud (if you can), repeat the words to yourself, and lean into how it feels in your body. Ready?

GROUP 1
Stress.
Stressed.
I am so stressed.
This is stressful!
I'm really stressed.

Now take a deep breath. Pull in lots of calming air and release slowly. As quickly as my words made you feel stressed, my words here are causing instant calm to wash over you and bring your body back to neutral. Do the same thing with the next group of words.

GROUP 2
Joy.
Happiness.
I am so joyous.
This brings me so much joy.
I have so much joy inside of me.

Where did you feel these feelings in your body? What do the feelings feel like? Emotions truly do feel different physically in the body. Learning how each emotion feels and where you feel it will help you notice it when that emotion comes up.

Self-awareness is the key to self-control. Once you are in control of yourself, you will stop getting in your own way! This is what will set you apart from others. You'll begin to notice that some people lack even a little self-awareness. People often act and react, letting their emotions lead them without much thought, and then they blame "life" for their shortcomings.

Picture yourself in a peaceful setting that doesn't stir up any strong emotions, positive or negative. Maybe you're relaxing in a café, watching TV, or reading a book. Take a moment to think of your own peaceful place.

This is your baseline. Remember it, so when you feel anything other than the feeling of being neutral, you'll know that there is an emotion involved. Negative emotions feel completely different to your baseline and should prompt you to become curious and explore how you are feeling.

Step 2: Naming the Singular Feeling
By labeling an emotion, we can create distance between ourselves and our experience, which allows us to *choose* how to respond to challenges. We are triggering our ability to use cognitive reappraisal here.

Here is the difference between using an emotion-avoiding statement versus successfully labeling an emotion:

Emotion-avoiding statement: What a terrible day!

Okay, it's been a bad day, but what are you really saying here? What are you *feeling* about this terrible day? What name would you give this feeling? Are you tired? Frustrated? Stressed? Angry? Sad? Referring to the weather? Who knows? Not me, because this emotion-avoiding statement doesn't tell me anything about how you *personally feel*. It just tells me that the day itself wasn't ideal.

Some other examples of emotion-avoiding statements that I hear often are:

- I've had enough!
- I'm sick of this
- F*ck this!
- This is bullsh*t!

When we use language like this, it feels like a release in the moment, but actually these types of expressions recycle the emotion! These phrases emphasize the overall negativity instead of pinpointing the emotion and truly working through it before letting it go. It doesn't release the emotion, it heightens it!

Labeling the emotion: I have *felt stressed* all day today.

Can you see how this sentence would not add fuel to the fire? It acknowledges your emotion but not from an emotive place. You are holding on to your rational and logical mindset. You are regaining control over what is happening in your body. You are putting the brakes on entering into the emotionally flooded state by naming the singular emotion!

But what if you are feeling more than one feeling at the same time? If you feel multiple emotions all at once, each one *is* still a singular feeling. Just name one at a time until you have separate identifiable emotions.

Sometimes I can feel overwhelmed *and* stressed, and then anxious because of those other two feelings! It is completely normal for feelings to daisy-chain in this way. You can still pinpoint what each feeling is, making each much more manageable than the jumble of unidentified emotions!

Looking at the next graphic, the mixing bowls represent our mind and emotions. In the first bowl, there are a bunch of mixed spaghetti-like emotions that feel unmanageable. They will most definitely lead to emotional flooding and dysregulation if left untangled. In bowl two, there are still the same emotions mixed together, but now you are being mindful of how your body is feeling. You have picked each emotion out and named them one by one.

This leaves you with the last bowl—the individual, unraveled, manageable emotions—making room for clear, logical thoughts.

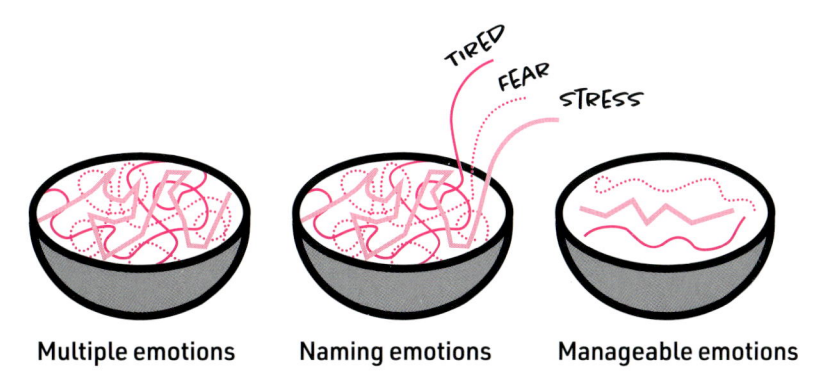

Multiple emotions   Naming emotions   Manageable emotions

Labeling the emotions: I have felt really *stressed* all day today, and then I felt really *frustrated* with myself for not feeling calm. I am feeling pretty *defeated* by it all.

You have three very clear emotions that you have become aware of and understand:

1. Stress
2. Frustration
3. Defeat

Step 3: Accepting What You Feel

In this fast-paced world, you're conditioned to quickly push past emotions, which leads you to wear your neurotypical mask tightly. This makes you ignore your feelings, even when you identify them, hoping to keep them hidden. I find this especially true in England, where I'm from. God forbid anyone sees me experiencing unpoised emotions!

Now that you've practiced identifying emotions that lead to dysregulation, it's time to focus on acceptance. Instead of resisting or hiding it, acknowledge its presence and sit with it. Acceptance allows for deeper understanding, self-compassion, and a stronger connection with yourself.

REFLECT AND ACT:
Can You Label Your Feelings Easily?

Labeling emotions can be challenging. We can feel them in our body but struggle to explain what they are!

Reflect

Many of us don't know our full range of emotions. We have eight primary emotions and an unmeasurable multitude of secondary and tertiary emotions that stem from them!

Act

The psychologist Gloria Willcox developed the "feelings wheel" in 1982. There have been many variations since, including my own! I have created a feelings wheel guide that includes the feelings wheel itself and the definitions for all 130 emotions!

I would have liked to include it in the book, but there are so many feelings on the wheel that the writing would be teensy-weensy! You can find it on my website: modernhippiemindset.com.

As you do, simply place your hand on your chest and say either in your head or out loud, "It's okay that I am feeling [*negative emotion*] right now."

Tune in to connecting with your younger self when you do this or shift your mindset to your best-friend perspective. You need reassurance that it is okay to have *big* feelings. It may be something that your younger self didn't get enough of, making this a lovely re-parenting practice too. You can add a slight nurturing rock to this also. Gently rock from side to side. You can give yourself a hug, which your inner child will love as a source of comfort in your time of need.

At this point of the self-soothing system, you have gone through steps one through three, and although they have taken time to explain in this chapter, they are worked through in quick succession in real life, as they are all thought-based steps. Your next step is a physical one.

Step 4: Choosing Your Next Physical Step

By now you have dodged dysregulation and you still have your logical brain working for you. So use it! Ask yourself, "What is my next step?" Here are some options:

STEPPING AWAY FROM THE STORM
- The conflict
- The task
- The space

STEPPING INTO THE CALM
- Outdoor walk
- Breath work
- Guided meditation, hypnosis, relaxing music

STEPPING TOWARD YOURSELF
- Journaling
- Self-love and care actions: treat yourself, connect to your inner child, tidy a space
- Rest: take a bath, lie down to collect your thoughts, take a timed nap.

The amazing thing here is it really *is* completely up to you because *you are still in control*! Now that you know how to take control and become calm, let's add some healthy dopamine back into your life!

The Most Important Things You Need to Know

- When it comes to controlling emotional dysregulation, remember to practice the Four-Step Self-Soothing System:

  Step 1: Notice what you feel and how it feels.
  Step 2: Name the singular feelings.
  Step 3: Accept what you feel.
  Step 4: Choose your next physical step.

The Dopamine Chase:
Seeking Happiness Healthily

A REGULAR JOKE IN THE ADHD COMMUNITY is how we are on a constant dopamine chase, but have you ever wondered why? Information is put out and passed around in the world, details get lost in translation, and the end result is only a surface-level summary of the original source.

People with ADHD struggle with *dopamine regulation*—specifically, the dopamine system, which is responsible for pleasure and reward, tends to be out of balance. This imbalance results in a sense of lacking reward, which can cause higher levels of stress.

Lower Dopamine and Higher Stress

I explained in chapter 11 that *emotional dysregulation* causes a *dysregulated nervous system*, and a dysregulated nervous system causes more moments of emotional dysregulation. Well, we now need to add *dopamine* into the mix so that we have the full picture.

Low dopamine causes you to have higher stress levels (and the potential to have a dysregulated nervous system), and this causes emotional dysregulation, which in turn lowers your dopamine. It all feeds into one another!

Looking at this at the genetic level, ADHD is linked to several faulty genes, including the DRD2 gene, which affects how neurons respond to dopamine. This impacts not only pleasure regulation but also your attention and focus. Essentially, these genetic factors mess with the brain's reward system, making everyday tasks feel less rewarding! A study published in *Neuropsychiatric Disease and Treatment*, a medical journal covering research in psychiatry and neurology, says:

> The problem lies in the genes that lay down the blueprint for manufacturing neurotransmitters. People with ADHD have at least one defective gene, the DRD2 gene that makes it difficult for neurons to respond to dopamine, the neurotransmitter that is involved in feelings of pleasure and the regulation of attention. Studies on genetic anomalies have implicated other dopaminergic genes such as the DRD4 receptor gene, the dopamine beta hydroxylase (DBH) gene, and the dopamine transporter genes as causative factors in ADHD.

To sum it up, ADHD is a complex disorder with genetic roots affecting neurotransmitter activity. This impacts dopamine rewards and heightens stress, making it challenging for those with ADHD to find balance and feel rewarded by everyday activities. Suddenly the doom piles of clothes in your bedroom are making sense.

Do You Chase Dopamine in Unhealthy Ways?

I don't want to drag you down with this information. Instead, I want to give you an evidence-based aha moment to validate you and boost your motivation to seek healthy dopamine! Having a gene that doesn't do its dopamine thing the way it's supposed to *of course* means you may have sought it in unhealthy ways. The study mentioned on the previous page repeatedly showed this predisposition can even lead to forming unhealthy addictions.

Some examples of unhealthy ways you may chase dopamine include:

Drug or alcohol abuse: Substance abuse, including nicotine and caffeine, can surge dopamine levels, reinforcing addictive behaviors.

Compulsive gambling: The excitement and anticipation of winning triggers dopamine release, reinforcing the urge to gamble.

Overeating: Foods high in sugar, fat, or salt can trigger dopamine release, leading to compulsive eating habits.

Excessive social media use: Constant notifications, likes, and comments can create a dopamine-driven cycle. I have to keep myself in check with this!

Risk-taking behaviors: Activities such as dangerous sports, reckless driving, law breaking, affairs, or thrill-seeking adventures spark dopamine levels.

Causing conflict: Conflict triggers the dopamine reward system by activating stress responses, anticipating positive outcomes, and reinforcing social validation or status. This engagement of the brain's reward pathways highlights how conflict, despite its negative aspects, can still prompt responses that are psychologically rewarding and motivating. The "ADHD rage" is suddenly making more sense now, right?

ADHD 101: Reward Deficiency Syndrome (RDS)

Reward deficiency syndrome (RDS) is a dysfunction in the brain's reward system. Dopamine is affected in individuals with genetic variants, particularly the DRD2 dopamine receptor gene—you know, the gene that the earlier study showed is defective in people with ADHD!

RDS shows up in different levels of severity, affecting people's ability to enjoy normal activities. The defect can drive you to engage in unhealthy activities that will increase your dopamine levels, such as substance abuse or binge eating. This genetic abnormality is also associated with aggressive behavior because that too stimulates the brain's use of dopamine!

→ WRITE IT DOWN: How Have *You* Been Chasing the Reward?

In your journal, reflect on your day-to-day life and make a list of how you have been getting your daily dose of dopamine. It can help break down your day into sections and write the activities in order, even if that means you repeat some of what is listed. This will give you a very honest overview. For example:

Morning
- Go on social media when I wake up
- Make a coffee
- Go back on social media
- Vape/smoke as I get ready
- Make toast
- Vape on my way to work
- Make another coffee
- Have a morning snack even though I'm not hungry

Afternoon
- Vape/smoke break before food
- Eat some chocolate after lunch even though I'm full
- Another coffee
- Scroll on social media between work tasks

Evening
- Snack after dinner
- Vape/smoke a lot
- Watch TV all night and check my phone during
- Have an alcoholic drink

Writing these activities can cause negative thoughts and emotions. Take a moment now to work through the Four-Step Self-Soothing System to avoid emotional dysregulation!

Step 1: Notice what you feel and how it feels.
Example: "I notice a heaviness in my stomach."
Step 2: Name the singular feeling.
Example: "I feel ashamed."
Step 3: Accept what you feel.
Example: "It's okay that I feel shame right now."
Step 4: Choose your next physical step.
Example: "I'm going to step toward myself and be self-loving."

REFLECT AND ACT: Boost Self-Love and Understanding by Reframing Your Experience

As you reflect on your examples of unhealthy dopamine chasing, it's important to comfort yourself. You now know why you have been doing this. You've been trying to make up for what your brain has been lacking. So, try to be loving, kind, empathic, and caring. For example:

> I did those things to make myself feel better. Now that I know how my brain works, it makes total sense, and I understand why I have been dopamine chasing in this way. It stems from me wanting to feel good. It's okay that I have been doing this. I love myself no matter what.

Now let's add to this by reframing your experience. We do this by focusing on how incredible your mind and body are. For example:

> It's pretty amazing that I had no idea that I have a gene that works differently and my body *knew* it was lacking something and tried to fix it. My brain learned how to get dopamine in the quickest and easiest ways, which is quite incredible! Now that I know what's going on, I can give myself healthy dopamine boosts!

Quick-Fix Dopamine Hits versus Slow-Releasing Dopamine

The goal is to retrain your brain to enjoy slow-releasing dopamine and transition away from quick-fix dopamine hits. That said, I'll share a few healthy quick-fix options too. So, what are the differences between slow- and quick-releasing dopamine? The quality of dopamine for one!

Dopamine Quality

A quick-fix dopamine hit surges your brain with an intense but short-lived rush. While these quick fixes provide an immediate sense of pleasure, they come with a harsh crash, leaving you feeling depleted and craving more!

On the other hand, slow-releasing dopamine from activities such as exercise, learning, or engaging in a creative hobby provides a more sustained and stable reward flow. These activities may not give you an instant high, but they keep you balanced and regulated.

Over time, your brain will learn to seek the slow release of dopamine in the same way it has learned to seek the quick fixes! Plus, with slow-releasing dopamine tasks you get the added bonus of a sense of pride and achievement. But we have ADHD and possibly the defective DRD2 gene, so let's look at a full dopamine menu next!

MINDSET RESET: Dopamine Detox versus Digital Detox

You may have heard of the rising dopamine detox trend, also known as "dopamine fasting." The idea is to reset your dopamine levels by reducing screen time, gaming, social media scrolling, and notification checking. Like most things, the science has gotten a little lost as the information has been passed around. Let's take a look at what dopamine fasting really is.

The Facts and The Fiction
- The dopamine fast was created by the psychologist Cameron Sepah, who advises that "the title's not to be taken literally."
- You *can't* fast from a naturally occurring brain chemical. Our brain may respond to social media and similar activities with dopamine, but detoxing from devices doesn't lower the accessible dopamine your brain can create. It just means the device hasn't triggered your reward system to respond.
- Dopamine fasting was created using cognitive behavioral therapy as its core methodology. The idea is that a person becomes less controlled by modern tech and chooses to avoid the unhealthy stimuli from notifications, likes, buzzes, and beeps.
- The purpose of the dopamine fast is to direct ourselves away from short-lived dopamine rewards and allow our brain to take breaks from the addictive stimulation.

To sum up, dopamine fasting is a quick-fix fast that gets you to detox the addictive behaviors, but you are not detoxing the dopamine itself because you can get dopamine in other ways! I highly recommend a *digital detox* while you lean into the slow-releasing dopamine boosts. Put your phone on Do Not Disturb, read in bed instead of scrolling, and go out into the *real* world that the digital world is making you miss!

Dopamine Menu: Order the Healthy Option

The dopamine menu concept comes from a 2020 YouTube video by Jessica McCabe, and I just love this way of selecting how we dopamine chase! Think of it as having a menu of items that you can choose to order your dopamine from.

Starters

These are the *healthy quick fixes* when you're craving an immediate taste of dopamine!

One-minute movement: Bursts of jumping up and down, skipping, dancing.

Music: Listen to high-energy music. Singing and dancing along is a triple threat for dopamine release.

A healthy snack: Fruit is the best healthy quick-fix food option because of its natural sweetness. Avoid using junk food as a quick fix!

Stretch-and-reset exercise: A few yoga poses or just stretching can bring a sudden surge of feeling reenergized.

A word-based game: Word searches, crosswords, and Wordle are great energizing options. Set a timer for a few minutes and complete as much as you can. I never regret when I smash a Wordle puzzle in less than a few minutes!

Cold-water therapy: A quick one-minute face plunge or switching your warm shower to cold at the end is a great sudden dopamine boost!

Cuddles: Whether it be a hug from a friend, a partner, or a pet, cuddling is a lovely and quick way to boost your dopamine levels.

Deep breathing exercises: Deep breathing can give you a natural uplifting high!

Laughter therapy: Even forcing yourself to laugh for a brief moment can create a positive shift in your brain chemistry!

Sides

Choose a side dish of dopamine when you are completing less-tasty low-dopamine tasks! Since a defective DRD2 gene decreases the availability of dopamine for everyday tasks, side orders are a must-have!

Upbeat focus music: For tasks that need full focus, instrumental upbeat music with isochronic tones can help. Isochronic tones are rhythmic stimuli that turn on and off quickly, engaging your brain. It makes boring tasks feel more stimulating.

Fidget stimming: Using a fidget tool adds needed stimulation to dull tasks. It also boosts focus, helping you complete tasks that slowly release dopamine.

Podcasts: Like TV, social media, and learning, podcasts give you a dopamine boost. They're perfect for chores that need physical effort but minimal mental focus.

Gamifying tasks: Games release plenty of dopamine, so turning tasks into a game is a great hack! You can do this by setting timed challenges. You make the rules!

Body double: Working alongside someone or chatting with them while doing a dull task can add a nice side order of dopamine through stimulating conversations and laughter.
Checklist: A checklist gives a rewarding feeling upon completion. Checking off each item gives you repeated dopamine boosts and a sense of accomplishment.

Mains

These main dish items create slow-releasing dopamine. They are the activities you should indulge in a little more because you will feel sustained after. I recommend doing one of these daily!

Exercise: There are many options for different ability levels. For the able-bodied beginner, a quick-paced walk. For the gym-goer, try running! For those less able, YouTube is home to a range of seated exercises. I used them myself when I broke my leg!
Cold-water therapy: Take a full-body plunge into a cold-water therapy tub or even in a natural body of water.
Gratitude journaling: Neuroscientific research says that dopamine and serotonin are released in our brains when we express gratitude.
Guided meditation: I suggest *guided* rather than just stand-alone meditation because I know how your ADHD mind wanders. Search for guided meditations that actively encourage feelings of happiness, joy, love, and gratitude for your dopamine reward.
Gardening and grounding: Digging in the dirt really does boost dopamine. The soil itself has microbes that stimulate serotonin production when inhaled. Completing a garden project triggers your reward response too. You really can grow your own dopamine!
Hobbies and learning: Whether it's crocheting, stand-up paddleboarding, jiujitsu, or collecting antiques . . . *anything* that isn't unhealthy that provides you with a sense of achievement will trigger your dopamine reward system.

Desserts

These are the indulgent dopamine treats. I don't want to demonize quick-fix dopamine hits, as we live in a world full of temptations. The list includes common options to be enjoyed in moderation. Too much cake causes a sugar crash!

> Scrolling on social media
> Coffee and drinking alcohol (although I recommend a caffeine- and
>   alcohol-free life for your ADHD brain)
> Watching TV
> Gaming
> Shopping
> And of course . . . Literal desserts!

Just remember that all of these are designed to be as addictive as possible!

Today's Specials!

These are the once-in-a-while options. They don't come up on the menu often, but when you can, try to squeeze them into your busy life to have a full dopamine day!

Spa day: Although a spa's main goal is to relax its visitors, it often comes with a bunch of dopamine-releasing moments especially when visited with friends! Once my sister-in-law and I had uncontrollable giggles when we plunged ourselves into the cold-water therapy pool. Most recently I went along with my nephew Freddie, who even made the "relaxing" citrus pool that was filled with floating lemons a hilarious experience. Suddenly we were trying to sink all the floating lemons and catching any of the escapees!

A dinner out: The combination of good food and good company is a really wholesome way to boost your dopamine levels.

A vacation: Vacations are surrounded by moments of dopamine rewards. You often do a little shopping before you go and during! You have fun days out, laughter with family and friends, indulge a little with food, ground yourself on beaches, dunk yourself in cool seas for a natural cold-water therapy . . . the list goes on!

A movie or show: The dopamine reward depends on the movie or show because I have 100 percent fallen asleep inside movie theaters and even at a Broadway show. (*Phantom of the Opera* just wasn't my thing.) Try to see things that you *know* you'll enjoy.

Comedy club: Injecting laughter into your life is an absolute must. In fact, laughter therapy can be a main-course item on your dopamine menu. It seems to me that negativity can't exist in our body when we laugh.

Adrenaline days: Disclaimer* I DO NOT RECOMMEND ANY SUPER-SCARY AND UN-SAFE ADRENALINE-JUNKIE ACTIVITIES. (If you injure yourself, I don't want to be liable for that.) However, adrenaline days are adored by the ADHD community and for good reason. They give us so much dopamine! Seek out whatever works to give you that peak of excitement and huge sense of reward. For me it is theme-park days, cycling, nature swimming in rivers, kayaking, long-distance hiking (because of the mental challenge), exploring new areas, slacklining, high rope courses, and ziplining. I am adventurous, but I am not the jump-out-of-a-plane kind of adventurous!

→ WRITE IT DOWN: Design Your Dopamine Menu

You now have a full menu of dopamine dishes to choose from. Make a note of this menu, remove ones that don't resonate with you, and add some of your own to it!

As you do this, connect to your inner child by asking the following questions:

- What did I love to do as a child?
- What made me really excited when I was little?

You've already discovered that it's safe to unmask, and you can use this to your advantage when creating your dopamine menu. List activities that fully embrace your fun-loving, silly self, and you'll have no problem getting dopamine in healthy and joyous ways.

When I did this I rediscovered my love of art, dance, and . . . Disney! Now I shamelessly blast the songs and become a dopamine-chasing princess! I draw and paint whenever I feel like I have been lacking in dopamine. I include dance in my everyday life by letting myself dance around the house like I used to as a little girl.

Asking myself these questions reminded me that I also have *always* loved exploring, especially when I pair it with a treasure-hunting theme! So I added magnet fishing, metal detecting, and antique shopping to my personalized dopamine menu.

I am and always have been a social person, and I need close connections to boost my dopamine levels. I know connecting with others can sometimes be difficult to navigate, but it's one of the best ways to get your daily dose of dopamine. I'm going to help you navigate all things "peopley" next!

The Most Important Things You Need to Know

- Lower dopamine result in higher stress levels, which can lead to emotional dysregulation.
- People with ADHD have at least one defective gene, the DRD2 gene that makes it difficult for neurons to respond to dopamine.
- Reward deficiency syndrome (RDS) is a dysfunction in the brain's reward system due to genetic variants, particularly in the DRD2 dopamine receptor gene.
- Slow-releasing dopamine is better for you than quick-fix dopamine hits.

Navigating Relationships with ADHD:
Tools to Connect One-on-One

THIS IS THE CHAPTER that you'll want to read out loud to your friends and family. However, you'll need to put your ego in check because I won't shy away from the challenging aspects of ADHD and relationships. Your ego protects you from feelings such as embarrassment and shame, but sometimes you need to override it and let yourself be vulnerable in order to grow.

By now you've learned how complex ADHD emotions can be. You're probably already aware that this can negatively impact relationships. But what about the less emotional ADHD symptoms? How do they impact your relationships? I've found that time blindness can make it difficult to stick to arranged plans, rejection sensitive dysphoria makes taking any feedback from friends and family an extremely hard pill to swallow, not to mention communication issues, struggling to pay attention, and impulsiveness. All of this can affect how you relate to others.

Why Stable Relationships Are Hard for ADHDers

A community of hundreds of thousands of ADHDers engage with my social media content on this tricky topic. The consensus? Relationships can feel boring! *Yikes!* Is this you? This is definitely one of the harder truths to consider, but let's look at this hidden shadow part of yourself.

I discovered after brutally honest self-reflection (and sharing it with the ADHD community) that I had a pattern of being in chaotic relationships, both romantically and platonically. The big question? How much of that has to do with me, and how much of it has to do with those who treated me badly? Let's take a closer look.

Who Is Causing the Chaos?

ADHDers often make quick connections because we tend to wear our hearts on our sleeves and lead with total honesty and familiarity. Unfortunately for us, when this is reciprocated, we assume that they are being innocently overly honest and familiar, just as we are. But this means we often miss signs of love bombing, a tactic used to gain trust quickly that is associated with narcissistic tendencies. Narcissists use love bombing to manipulate others, quickly creating a false sense of intimacy and security to fulfill their own needs for control and validation while masking their true intentions.

Additionally, people with ADHD may have novelty-seeking tendencies, craving new experiences and stimulation for excitement. This can lead us into relationships that aren't suited to us. The thrill of a new relationship can make us miss all the red flags!

These two aspects of our personalities mean we often experience toxic relationships. Four out of the five serious relationships I have been in have been toxic (chaotic in nature, argumentative, emotionally abusive, or physically abusive).

It's true that no one is immune to experiencing toxic relationships, but having ADHD makes us particularly vulnerable to experiencing emotional abuse. This can take the form of manipulation tactics such as love bombing, gaslighting, guilt-tripping, charm, flattery, isolation, passive aggression, and so on.

Once a person experiences this sort of continued stress, their body becomes accustomed to it. As we learned earlier, ADHDers can quite literally become stress addicts and find comfort in chaos, and this extends to our relationships. If this is what we are used to, healthy relationships can feel somewhat boring by comparison. This is where you have to take responsibility if you too have accidentally normalized toxicity and now transfer that onto healthy relationships.

How Does Your Attachment Style Impact Your Relationships?

Your attachment style forms the foundation of your relationships, so understanding and navigating your style is crucial to your ADHD Reset journey! Here are the four attachment styles:

Secure attachment: You view yourself and others positively, feel comfortable with intimacy, and communicate well in relationships.

Anxious-preoccupied attachment: You often have a negative self-view but a positive view of others, leading to feeling "less than," a fear of rejection, and a constant need for approval. Relationships often make you feel anxious, unsafe, and insecure.

Dismissive-avoidant attachment: You view yourself positively but others negatively, avoiding closeness due to fear of losing independence; you often pull away and avoid conflict. This can cause inner conflict as you desire closeness but struggle with it.

Fearful-avoidant attachment: You have negative views of yourself and others, desiring closeness but fearing hurt and struggling with trust. Relationships may feel chaotically confusing; you alternate between fear and avoidance ("hot and cold" behavior).

Common ADHD Attachment Styles

If you have ADHD, you're more likely to develop insecure attachment styles.

ANXIOUS-PREOCCUPIED ATTACHMENT

Impulsivity and the need for immediate gratification, which are common with ADHD, can lead you to seek constant reassurance and approval. The good news is you're already working on getting slower dopamine peaks and gravitating away from immediate gratification, which will help with anxious-preoccupied attachment tendencies. You're also learning the value of self-kindness, connecting with your inner child and higher self, and adopting a best-friend perspective for support. This self-reliance reduces the need for external validation, as you now know how to validate yourself.

FEARFUL-AVOIDANT ATTACHMENT

Your emotional dysregulation and inconsistent behavior patterns associated with ADHD may have resulted in negative relationships. You may desire closeness but also fear intimacy, causing the fearful-avoidant attachment style.

However, after getting better at regulating your emotions, you will feel safer within relationships because you're less likely to seek chaos, cause conflict, and act on heightened emotions that have affected you in the past.

ADHD 101: What's *Your* Attachment Style?

If you still aren't sure which attachment style you have, take the quick flowchart quiz to figure it out:

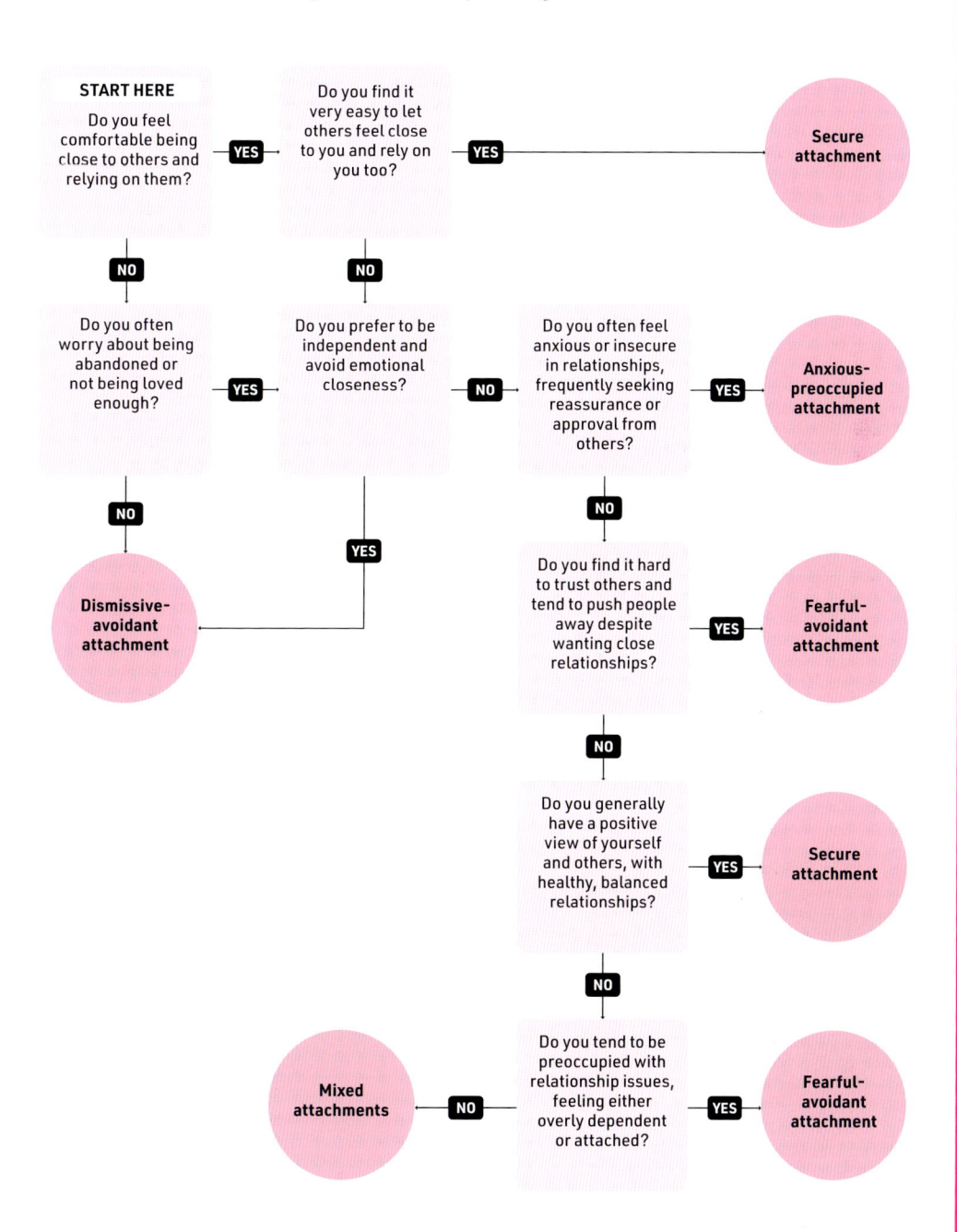

Emotional Regulation within Relationships

Did you know that during conflict we're triggered to feel like it's a life-or-death situation? That's why people often find it incredibly difficult to drop an argument or be proven wrong. Part of us literally feels like we might die! We need to remind our outdated nerves that this is not the case. In the twenty-first century, we aren't dueling with swords. Instead, we're probably typing an angry text from the safety of our own home! This means we often have time and space on our side to self-regulate when we have heightened emotions.

Previously I explained the four-step self-soothing system as:
>Step 1: Notice what you feel and how it feels.
>Step 2: Name the singular feeling.
>Step 3: Accept what you feel.
>Step 4: Choose your next physical step.

When it comes to self-regulation with relationships, I've added a much needed step to stay calm during conflict.

The Five-Step Self-Soothing System with Relationships
>Step 1: Notice what you feel and how it feels.
>→ **Step 2: Pause to process.**
>Step 3: Name the singular feeling.
>Step 4: Accept what you feel.
>Step 5: Choose your next physical step.

When your emotions are heightened in the company of others, you're at increased risk of dysregulation. You can spiral because of added pressure and have a meltdown that appears to be out of proportion to the problem the person has presented to you. Step 2 of this five-step system will stop you in your tracks, giving you the time you need before you respond. Remember, we don't need to immediately swipe back. We are not in a duel!

In person you can say, "I need time to process this," politely pausing the conversation so you can work through your self-soothing system. Over text, you can close or mute your phone (technology sometimes works in our favor) so you can process before replying. With practice I'm now much better at this, but occasionally I react instead of using step 2. When this happens, first I comfort my ego, who is afraid of embarrassment, by letting myself know that I am safe. I then explain to myself, "I didn't give myself time to process this and reacted with emotions that I hadn't realized I was feeling. What I would like to say instead is, 'This has made me feel . . .'"

Of course, you can also apologize if you feel you need to! The goal here is to get your sense of self-control back! It's something that not many people have during conflict, ADHD or not! Learning this self-soothing system in relationships is a superpower!

Communication Is Key, and So Are Intentions

While the additional self-soothing step encourages you to pause so that you have time to process, eventually you'll want to express how you feel because all conflict resolution relies on communication. Silently pushing feelings down results in stress being stored in the body, bitterness toward the other person, and distance growing between you. It can be a scary step to take because it means you have to be vulnerable, and it's possible that you may be rejected. The way to navigate this? *More* communication!

The Three-Step Communication System

1. Tell the person your intention—for example, "I want to resolve this with you."
2. Be reassuring so they know that they, too, are not facing rejection: "Your friendship means the world to me, and I don't want to lose you."
3. Explain *your root emotions*—the vulnerable feelings that you may be hiding or masking with anger. This is when using the feelings wheel works wonders!

Some feelings that can present as *anger* are:

- Disappointment
- Humiliation or embarrassment
- Fear of losing someone
- Betrayal
- Jealousy

- Guilt
- Shamed
- Judgment
- Insecurity
- Hurt

Look at how different these two sentences are:

Dysregulated and ego led: "I am so f*cking angry with you! How dare you talk to me like that? Who do you think you are?! You are an awful person . . ."
Regulated and vulnerable: "I really want to resolve this with you. I reacted earlier without processing how I felt. I didn't mean to be unkind. I don't want to lose you. But the way you spoke to me earlier made me feel disrespected and it hurt me . . ."

Out of the two, which do you think is going to get a more positive response?

I can sense some eyerolls! I *know* all too well that not everyone is going to respond well to your new regulated conflict-resolution-seeking self. This is when I tap back in touch with my higher self to guide me toward the best resolution.
I ask myself the following questions:

- Is this a one-time thing or is this person continuously causing me to have negative experiences and feelings?
- Do I want to keep exchanging my energy with this person?
- Do I *have* to resolve this or can I walk away? (Because sometimes we have to, right?)

After repeatedly experiencing a friend's unkind behavior and emotionally manipulative tactics such as passive aggression and gaslighting, I overcame my fear of rejection and directly asked if I had done something to upset them. I reassured them of my love for them and how much they meant to me, and I encouraged them to be completely honest with me. They insisted I'd done nothing wrong, yet the jabs, swipes, and digs continued, leaving me no longer feeling responsible. I had been honest, but it wasn't reciprocated. Not everyone can ditch their ego to meet in harmony. After receiving another unkind message *on my birthday*, I decided this friendship no longer served me. Through tears I promised my husband I would never exchange my energy with them again.

Setting boundaries and standing in your power like this gets easier to do the more you increase your sense of self-love and self-worth. However, it still can feel like a big loss and trigger the feeling of rejection.

Overcome Rejection Sensitive Dysphoria

Rejection sensitive dysphoria (RSD) often occurs alongside ADHD. This means that you are extremely sensitive to any hint of criticism or rejection. If you have RSD, you may react strongly in situations where you feel you're being ignored or not valued. This sensitivity can affect how you handle relationships and daily life, sometimes causing you to avoid situations that might trigger these feelings.

I recommend shifting your mindset in these moments. For instance, writing a book comes with a surplus of edits, feedback, and constructive criticism, and we can't always tailor the way in which it's delivered to us. At the very start of the process, I found it very challenging not to take it personally.

The publishing process made every insecurity I have bubble up, and I tried to avoid reviewing edits for as long as possible. I knew what I needed to do, but putting it into practice took courage. I needed to coach myself through each moment.

How to Deal with Feedback or Criticism

Dealing with people at work isn't easy. Feedback in the workplace is not only unavoid-able but essential. During times of receiving feedback on your work, coach yourself with chosen thoughts, such as:

- They are *helping* me.
- Their feedback is *supportive*.
- The constructive criticism is to *help me*.
- I can receive feedback and be *great at my job* at the same time.

It's important to use words that spark a sense of being cared for, to shift your perspec-tive from feeling judged and in fear to supported and free from harsh self-criticism.

Negative feedback from loved ones is an even harder pill to swallow. If my husband points out that I have done something to hurt his feelings, a huge sense of guilt, shame, and fear of rejection can wash over me. I have to very carefully navigate the situation to avoid spiraling into an unnecessary place of despair. I choose to have thoughts like:

- He feels *so safe* with me that he can share what he feels.
- I share my feelings with him and *I want him to* do the same with me.
- He *loves me* so much that he wants to resolve this.
- I am still a *good person* and he still *loves me* very much.

At both home and work, the main goals of your chosen thoughts are to remind yourself of your strengths regardless of the feedback, to reassure yourself that the feedback is for your benefit, and to keep your self-worth intact!

The Best Way to Request Feedback

Adjusting how you receive feedback can be transformational. If you are comfortable with someone, try asking them to deliver feedback in this format:

1. Say something positive.
2. Say something negative (the constructive criticism).
3. Say something positive.

I call this the "positive poo sandwich"! It just softens the blow when getting feedback that can trigger feelings of rejection. My husband and I are still working on this one, but I have no shame saying, "Can you check this for me? But give me a positive poo sandwich, please!"

Detox Daily Comparisons

Unchallenged RSD can commonly make us compare ourselves to others and hold ourselves to extremely unrealistic expectations. Do a detox of the daily comparisons!

1. **Have a feel-good social media feed.** Accounts that make you reflect negatively on yourself without giving you a boost of encouragement simply cause your self-worth to plummet regularly. Ditch them!
2. **Have a self-focused attitude.** Whenever you begin to compare yourself to others, you put yourself down and lift others up. Be mindful, press pause, then list three things about yourself that make you feel a sense of pride. It can even help to consider what parts of yourself others would like to adopt.
3. **Become curious about the comparison.** Why are you comparing yourself? It may reveal a hidden desire . . .

Use Jealousy as a Growth Tool!

When you compare and feel jealous, get curious and shift this from an uncomfortable moment to a powerful growth tool. Ask yourself, "What *exactly* is making me jealous? What am I looking at here that I desire?" This reframes jealousy and turns it into a positive moment of self-reflection and discovery.

It's Okay to Ask for Help: How to Communicate Your Needs

Now that you have tools to handle feedback, let's learn to communicate your needs in every area of your life! This does not make you needy, weak, or less than anyone else. It makes you stronger! Have you ever seen someone say, "I need *this* to do *that*," and thought, "Wow—they're weak"? Or did you think, "Holy poop, they're confident!" Asking for what you need is a boss move.

I live by "If you don't ask, you don't get!" I have received many things by asking for them, including support from loved ones, colleagues, and even strangers. For example, if you are studying and you need the extra prep time before the exam, ask for it. If you are at work and need a different chair that lets you move around more, ask for one. If you are struggling with the laundry at home, ask for help.

Especially if you need emotional or physical support to help you with your ADHD, you go get it! I have needed herbalists, nutritionists, talk therapists, hypnotherapists, life coaches, business coaches, editors, authors, agents, colleagues, friends, my parents, my partner—all to support me. There is no shame in seeking support.

How to Communicate: Ten Talking Tools

Having ADHD can make communication challenging. Sometimes we speak too much, sometimes not at all. Sometimes we listen with an intense eye stare, and other times we haven't heard a single word! Below are ten tools to help you communicate:

1. **The nodding dog:** Nod along as someone speaks to keep your focus on them.
2. **Ask questions:** Becoming curious in conversation keeps you on track, makes conversations more interesting, and improves your engagement.
3. **Follow-ups:** After verbal conversations, ask for follow-up emails or texts to make sure you understand everything.
4. **Scheduled resolution:** Schedule time to talk about "serious matters" with loved ones. You both enter the conversation seeking resolution and have preprocessed what you are going to bring to the table.
5. **Scheduled catch-ups:** Set regular phone calls with family and friends.
6. **Background beats:** When relaxing with friends, it helps me to have a little background noise on. I feel less uncomfortable during pauses.
7. **Meeting talking points:** Before work meetings or friend meetups, make talking points to talk through everything you want. I hate nothing more than leaving a friend and thinking, "Crap! I forgot to ask about X."
8. **Parroting:** Repeat back what you heard to confirm understanding. Example: "Did I understand that right? You said . . ."
9. **Use "I feel" statements:** Expressing your feelings isn't accusatory and often helps avoid causing further conflict.
10. **Use "I need" statements:** Express your needs clearly. Add in the why to make it even clearer. Example: "I need five minutes to process so I can regulate."

The Most Important Things You Need to Know

- ADHD makes us particularly vulnerable to experiencing emotional abuse and toxic relationships.
- If you have ADHD, you're more likely to develop insecure attachment styles.
- Pause to process during conflict: "I need time to process this."
- Request feedback as a "positive poo sandwich!"

15

Making Life Easier:
Managing the Once Unmanageable

LIFE WITH ADHD CAN BE PRETTY CHAOTIC if we don't have the right management tools to feel organized and in control. This is the chapter you may want to grab a highlighter for and make notes on the most!

Our days can fly by with multiple half-finished tasks, ignored chores, and a constant feeling of urgency caused by always falling behind with things. Even that sentence sounds chaotic and overwhelming! In the exact way we looked at your emotionally flooded brain and simplified it by looking at the singular feelings, you are going to have a perspective shift here and simplify your life.

"How Can This Be Easier?"

This simple question helps me with every single task I do! For example, recording videos for my social media can feel like a lot of effort! I need the bright lights, I have to plug them in, position them, get my tripod out, position that, do my makeup, think of a topic, script it . . . the list goes on! But by asking "How can this be easier?" I have taken this overly complex task and made it something I do every day with total ease.

"How can this be easier?" prompts you to ask more questions that guide you through the simplification of tasks. Do I *need* camera lights or can I just stand by my bright bedroom window? Do I *need* a tripod for this or can I just hold my phone? Do I *need* a word-for-word script or could I just start speaking and see how it flows?

If you follow me, you'll know I am not BS'ing you right now because 90 percent of my videos are of me standing by my bedroom window, holding my phone, and they all feel unscripted . . . because they are. Could I make them extra profesh? Absolutely. Do I *need* to in order to get the task done? Nope.

Simplifying = Smaller Steps That Are Easier to Do

But this isn't about cutting corners. Sometimes simplifying something means breaking a task into smaller steps that feel easier to achieve. Asking "How can this be easier?" has had a huge impact on my ability to not only start a task but get it done. Suddenly what felt like an overwhelming, overcomplicated job becomes easy-breezy to achieve, and you can do this for *everything*, such as:

- Making a morning routine that includes brushing your teeth and washing your face
- Making breakfast, lunch, and dinner
- Packing a bag . . . Remember this example from earlier in the book?

Use the Five Control Questions to Relieve Stress Related to Tasks

In chapter 12, you learned the four-step self-soothing system and the five control questions. If asking yourself how to make the task easier didn't work, this is when you should use those control questions. Tasks can so often feel like overwhelming stressors to us. This is your reminder to get curious if you need to and investigate *why*.

→ WRITE IT DOWN: Five Control Questions

Here is a reminder to write down the five control questions that you ask yourself when a task or situation feels like a stressor:

1. Why does this feel stressful to me?
2. Have I done this or something similar successfully before?
3. Is the task achievable?
4. What parts of the task do I anticipate I'll struggle with?
5. What can I do to make it easier for myself?

Answering the fifth question in this exercise leads us back to the question at the heart of this chapter and how to make your life easier.

Use Light Language When You Talk to Yourself

In chapter 10 we looked at ditching negative brain stimulation, and I mentioned using heavy language and light language. When you're doing a task, it's important to remember this distinction.

Heavy language is often used to initiate tasks by saying things like:

- I *have* to . . .
- I *need* to . . .
- I have *got to* . . .

Language like this triggers you to have a sense of urgency and peaks your stress levels, giving you the perception of the task being more stressful than it often is.

Swapping the way you speak about your to-do list is more powerful than you may realize. This morning, for instance, I felt the pressure of writing this exact chapter because I had a couple of days off from work this week. I caught myself saying, "I *need* to get the chapter done!" But then swapped it to "I *get to* write a new chapter today!"

You can melt resistance and initiate tasks with so much more ease by using light language like:

- I *really want* to . . .
- I *get to*. . .
- *I am* going to . . .

I have practiced light language so much that I turn these moments into times to feel incredibly grateful. Earlier today I didn't just say, "I get to write a new chapter." I went on to think about how amazing it is that I was once a young girl with a dream of being an author, and now I get to spend my day doing work that I used to spend hours and hours doing for free, wishing that someone would one day read my words! I even started feeling grateful when it comes to cleaning my home, because once you say, "I *get* to clean my house," you realize in that moment how truly lucky you are to have a home to clean!

With practice you can learn to automatically simplify each task, search for a stressor if you feel resistance, and use light language instead of heavy language.

But sometimes it actually might be an easy task. You might not even feel like the task is stressful, but you *still* can't bring yourself to do it! Let's look at why that is.

Why Can't You Just Do It?

Here are three main suspects for why you can't seem to complete a task:

1. **Executive dysfunction:** Executive dysfunction involves challenges in the mental processes that help with organizing thoughts and activities, prioritizing tasks, managing time, and making decisions.
2. **Demand avoidance:** People with pathological demand avoidance (PDA) avoid complying with demands. The demand avoidance can be associated with high levels of anxiety. The demands can be:

   - **External:** Imposed by others, like a deadline or an instruction from a colleague
   - **Internal:** Imposed by *yourself*, like a new routine, commitment, or task
   - **Explicit:** A direct demand—"Have it on my desk in an hour!"
   - **Implicit:** A polite and reasonable request or unsaid expectation— "Would you mind cleaning your dishes when you have finished dinner please?"

3. **Task paralysis:** ADHD paralysis is not a medical diagnosis but a commonly experienced symptom of ADHD. It happens when you are overwhelmed by your environment or the amount of information you are having to process. It puts you in an avoidant freeze state.

There are a number of difficulties that can be extracted from the above three primary reasons we struggle to "just do it." Let's work through each specific block!

Organize Your Thoughts

Using the five control questions and light language will already help with organizing your thoughts, but sometimes your brain can still feel disorganized. Here are three ways to organize your busy brain:

1. **Brain dump:** Let every to-do that is in your mind pour out onto a page. Dump it all out.
2. **Manage the mess:** Once you have brain dumped, you'll still feel scattered, but at least the info is out of your mind and on paper in black and white. Next, turn this muddle of thoughts into easy-to-read bullet points.
3. **Regulate:** Be mindful of how you feel throughout and identify those singular emotions to keep your emotions regulated as you organize your tasks! If I notice the feeling of overwhelm in my body while I am brain dumping and reading everything I have (get) to do, I use the self-soothing system and often practice deep-breathing techniques.

I created the low cost OWNLY planner to help with this process. I was so sick of expensive hardback planners feeling overly precious! I used to feel guilty if I spelled a word wrong, crossed something out, or scribbled my to-do list in untidy handwriting. It honestly just made me feel more overwhelmed. This planner has a daily brain-dump section and different prompts to guide you to feel fully organized.

The OWNLY planner has the following sections included, but you can take inspiration from this format and use it in any notepad or digital planner you have.

My morning habits and tasks: This is for your unique, repetitive morning tasks.
The thing I've been putting off: Face the thing you feel most resistance toward. Without this prompt, I doubt you'd be reading a book written by me right now!
Today I am 100 percent going to . . . : Get real with yourself. That's why I only put five spaces in this category to help you set realistic expectations and avoid overwhelm.
Extra things I did that I want to write then check off just for the dopamine! You know I had to find a way to sneak in those extra hits of dopamine!
My evening habits and tasks: This is for your unique, repetitive evening tasks and includes "Plan Tomorrow" so that you'll feel in control when you wake up.

Categorize, Then Prioritize

I often slot my brain-dump tasks into the categories of my OWNLY planner and then number them after the fact. It stops me from feeling pressured to write my to-do list in the right order from the get-go! Stick a number next to it, and even if something else comes up, you only have to rewrite the numbers!

Here is an example of how I categorize and prioritize my to-dos. First I write the tasks into the category.

Morning Habits and Tasks
Unload dishwasher
Brush teeth/wash face
Go on a run
Shower and get ready

Then I add numbers:

Morning Habits and Tasks
2 Unload dishwasher
1 Brush teeth/wash face
3 Go on a run
4 Shower and get ready

You could do this yourself on a notepad by brain dumping, then writing four categories (morning, afternoon, evening, task I have been putting off), bullet-pointing your to-dos under each category, and then numbering them into a priority order.

What Is the Real Priority?

Some things need doing that day, and others are daily works in progress. However, executive dysfunction can make it difficult to make decisions and blur your vision when you review your to-dos. Try the HAPI method to prioritize and put things into perspective:

HAPI
- **H**as a deadline of today: These are the "urgent" tasks that should come first.
- **A**ppointments for that day: Even if the appointment is later in the day, plan for this first before you plan out the rest of your to-dos.
- **P**utting it off: The tasks you've been putting off should always get priority placement over the more general to-dos.
- **I** am working on it: These are your least-priority tasks. They do not have imminent deadlines but need daily doses of you working on them.

Manage Your Time

Time blindness is a motherfluffer for those with ADHD! We just don't seem to be able to keep track of time very easily, and we don't accurately estimate the time it takes us to do tasks! This is why you probably overwhelm yourself with too much to do.

Time Hacks

If you think it is going to take you thirty minutes to get ready, give yourself an hour. If you estimate that writing the important email will take five minutes, give yourself ten. If you think a project you're working on will take half a day, it will probably take the full day.

This isn't always accurate. I have doubled up the time for tasks and still run over! This just proves how much we underestimate how long tasks can take. The running theme here is things usually take longer than we expect. So maybe triple it!

How to Track Your Time

I know you have your phone attached to you at all times, but do you use it to keep track of the time as you are executing a task? Or do you check the time and then scroll through videos? Analog clocks are the *best* because you can see the passage of time! Plus you pick up your phone way less, so you keep on track with your task.

Digital Reminders

It's a common mistake to set a reminder for the time you need to leave the house for an appointment or when you have to start a task. You need task-transition time!

For instance, today I have a video meeting at 4:00 p.m. I set an alarm for 3:00 p.m. so I can transition from the task I'm doing and get ready. I set a second alarm for 3:30 p.m. to prompt me again (just in case I didn't move my butt), a 3:50 p.m. alarm to remind me to get drinks (yes, plural) before the meeting, and a 3:55 p.m. alarm to tell me to sit my ass down and click on the meeting link.

Is four alarms excessive? Absolutely not. It gives me so much mental freedom to know that I only have to think of this once—set the alarms and wait to be prompted!

Task Transitioning

The biggest time stealer is the time we lose when transitioning from one task to another. We finish a task at 2:12 p.m. and because it's not a nice round number, we give ourselves a little breakypoo, then suddenly—*WABAM!*—it's 3:45 p.m. and our to-do list got lost in a weird task-transitioning time warp!

First, we need our tasks to be prompted. Surprise, surprise—I am going to suggest again for you to use a planner or digital task app.

Here are five tips for handling task transitions:

1. Always have your phone alarm app on in the background of your phone. (You already have millions of unclosed tabs anyway, so make this a staple one!)
2. Play a song while you are taking a task-transitioning break. When the song ends, that is your prompt to move on to the next task on your to-do list.
3. Use music to guide you through your tasks. Decide the shower should take you no more than three full songs. Once the third song ends, you are prompted to get out of the shower and transition to the next step of your day.
4. Pomodoro timers are great to put you into a twenty-five minute focus and give you regular five-minute breaks. You can use this to not only take regular breaks and avoid burnout but also to prompt you to break from one task and be prompted to start another. I use these timers regularly when I really don't feel like sitting down to do administrative work. I am always in total disbelief when the timer pings to take a five-minute brain break.
5. If I find myself slipping into a freeze state when going from one task to the next, I use the very simple 1-2-3 method. I speak out loud, "One, two, three!" As soon as I say "three," I have made it nonnegotiable that I will get up and get back to my planned-out day.

Make Easier Decisions

We have already looked at how to prioritize and order your daily tasks, which will help you avoid decision fatigue, but each task requires lots of little decisions: What? When? Why? How?

Executive function is fully developed by age thirty. However, people with ADHD are often 30 to 40 percent delayed in executive function development, which can impair one or more of your circuits that help you make decisions.

Here is an overview of our main circuits:

The "What" Circuit: This circuit controls our working memory and visual processing, which helps us execute plans and work through the specific steps needed to complete tasks and projects.
The "When" Circuit: This circuit helps with organization, the timing and sequence of events, and the order we complete tasks.
The "Why" Circuit: This circuit is associated with understanding motives and intentions, and it affects our emotions. When impaired, it can impact how we think and feel about tasks.
The "How" Circuit: This circuit deals with the planning and execution of actions, and understanding what is involved in carrying out tasks.

Because these circuits may be impaired, you need to trigger your brain to use them. Ask the following questions:

1. **What** steps does this task require me to take? The key here is to be realistic with yourself about what the task involves.
2. **When** does this task need to be completed? This should help you put the task in priority order. Is it urgent or is it a task you are working on regularly without an immediate deadline?
3. **Why** is this important for me to do? This is to prompt you to self-motivate. For example, tidying up your workspace helps you think more clearly and avoid overstimulation.
4. **How** can I make this task easier? As you have already learned, this *really* helps.

Overcome Task Anxiety

I can't stress this enough: *PLAN YOUR DAYS!* Half of the anxiety you likely feel about a task is caused by having it in your mind as a repetitive sudden reminder popping in your brain: "OMG, I can't forget to do that!" The other half is likely caused by the language you use around the task: "I *need* to get that done!"

My planner is my second brain. I can write things down and let myself forget about it. I'm no longer demanding myself all day long to "Remember this" and "Quickly do that!" This means I avoid . . . demand avoidance! The planner doesn't demand from me; it supports me, guides me, and helps me to work through my to-do list without any anxious urgent feelings.

Remove the Environmental Overwhelm

Before leaving a room, practice the "use it, remove it, improve it" method I created: Use the room for whatever it is you are doing (watching TV, eating dinner, working out), then *remove* and put away the items you added into that space. Finally, *improve* the space: neaten the sofa cushions you were sitting on, fold the throw, and so forth.

Organize Information to Avoid Overwhelm

You've learned the value of using a planner or digital to-do lists, but you can't always plan for an information dump from someone else! Say you're working on a project and get an email from a colleague that contains a lot of information. Suddenly you feel overwhelmed. What now?

The key here is to look for *hidden* tasks! Reading this new bulk load of information is a task in itself, so this needs adding to your to do list.

Next you need to be *realistic* about the time it takes to go through the information, and then reorder your tasks to fit this in.

Okay. Now that you have handled that, you can look at how to literally organize bulk-sized information. This really is down to you and your preferences, but letting the information get lost in your emails is not going to cut it anymore—not if you want to be the new calm and collected you!

I use a workspace platform called Trello that lets me create multiple to-do lists in one space. Each to-do list has different "cards," and within each card I can write text, make clickable to-do lists, include links, save files, add deadlines, and so forth. I absolutely do not know how I would manage writing a book, my business—my Christmas gift lists, even—if it was not for Trello. I'm not being paid to talk about them; in fact, they don't even know I exist (except perhaps my email being on one of their huge user databases)!

There are lots of workspaces like this that you can use, but my recommendation is definitely this one. Just don't freak out when you first open it. Watch their how-to videos, sit back, and relax knowing that you have finally found something to store everything that your busy brain simply cannot!

As your tasks become easier and time is saved as a result, you will make room for all those new healthy habits you've always wanted to implement. Next, I'll show you exactly how you can form lasting habits and achieve your goals!

The Most Important Things You Need to Know

- Use light language when thinking and talking about your tasks: I *really want* to, I'd *like* to, I *get to*. . .
- Simplify your tasks and shift into a growth mindset by asking, "How can this be easier?"
- Categorize your tasks (morning, afternoon, evening, things you've been putting off), and then prioritize them with numbers.
- Make task-based decisions by triggering your circuits with "What? Why? When? How?"
- Methods to practice:
  - **Use it, remove it, improve it:** Use this method to reduce environmental overwhelm.
  - **1-2-3 move method:** Use this method to help with task initiation and transitioning.
  - **HAPI:** Order your to-do lists in priority order with this method: **H**as a deadline of today, **A**ppointments for that day, **P**utting it off, **I** am working on it.

Take Control:
Build Better Habits to Achieve Your Goals

WITHOUT HEALTHY HABITS AND STRUCTURE, you are living with unmanaged ADHD symptoms. When you mindlessly muddle through your day, your stress levels will increase. Increased stress equals worsened ADHD symptoms! This is why healthy habits are vital for you. So let's take control by building better habits to achieve your goals.

How Long Do Habits Take to Form?

It takes anywhere between 18 to 254 days to form a new habit, with an average of 66 days. Sixty-six days is just over two months, and 254 days is eight months plus a bit more. If you feel you struggle to make lasting habits, I'm sure you're thinking now that you will need the full eight-plus months! I'm here to call you out on that!

I bet you have had a few unhealthy habits that you formed quicker than the average of sixty-six days and maintained them! For instance, checking your phone when you don't need to, scrolling on social media in bed, eating unhealthy foods, watching TV every night instead of doing something healthier for your brain.

I bought my husband a phone holder for the shower. I thought he would enjoy listening to his audiobooks while showering. It was an innocent and healthy purchase. One day I decided to watch an episode of *Friends* while showering, then I did it the next day, and then the next. It took a grand total of one single day for it to become a habit that I now have to reverse!

→ **WRITE IT DOWN: What Are Your Good and Bad Habits?**
Jot down a few existing habits that you already have. They can be good or bad. Then try to estimate how long each took to become automatic.

This practice is not to shame you for the unhealthy habits you have—we all have some! It is to highlight the fact that you have the ability to form new habits very quickly. It is all about the reward you get from them!

Unhealthy Habits versus Healthy Habits

There is a reason why your unhealthy habits feel so much easier to implement than the healthy ones!

Take a look at the chart to see the differences between the two:

Healthy Habits	Unhealthy Habits
Rely on external cues and triggers	Triggered internally by cravings
Rely on decision-making and choosing to take action	Easier to be automated because cravings surge us into action
Slow dopamine–releasing tasks	Quick dopamine fix
Increase well-being	Lower well-being

As you can see, healthy habits rely on external cues, which means they require effort. Things like alarms, prompts, planning, and decisions are involved. Whereas the unhealthy habits are mostly triggered by internal cravings. For example, when a smoker internally craves their next cigarette, or when you suddenly crave the dessert on the menu even though you are physically full.

Healthy habits are, for the most part, in the slow dopamine–releasing category, meaning that you don't get a sudden hit of dopamine like you do with unhealthy habits. A ten-minute walk, for instance, makes you feel good, but it takes ten minutes instead of the two seconds it takes to eat a chocolate!

The main difference I want you to focus on here is that healthy habits increase your overall well-being and unhealthy habits lower it. Really, it is all about overriding the instant gratification and making peace with the delayed gratification.

This chart shows you the different outcomes between choosing healthy habits, which have a delayed gratification, versus unhealthy habits, which have an instant gratification.

Healthy Habits	Unhealthy Habits
Better brain rewards	Addictive dopamine spikes
Sense of achievement	Sense of failing, guilt, and shame
Increased self-pride, confidence, and trust	Lowered self-worth, confidence, and belief
Improved health	Worsened health

ADHD: Keeping It Simple

The habit loop consists of three key components:

1. **The cue or craving:** This is what triggers the habit. If you have a planner on your desk, it triggers you to plan your day, while a craving triggers you to eat something sugary, smoke, and things like that.
2. **The response:** The behavior that you respond with when you have the cue or craving.
3. **The reward:** The feel-good-feeling that you get from the action you have taken.

Understanding the habit loop can really help you form new habits. You can plant new cues to trigger a new behavior and get more rewards.

The irony of this is you will be doing every single one of your current unhealthy habits to feel good, but they actually make things worse in the long run. So, please be very kind to yourself while reflecting on your unhealthy habits and lack of healthy habits. Your body and brain are very clever and have figured out how to feel good fast. However, they lack understanding of the lasting effects!

Remove the Pressure

Forming new habits can feel like a lot of pressure, especially now knowing it can take over eight months to become automatic. This can paint a picture that you *have to be perfect* for eight months straight; and if you skip a day, you have just wasted all your efforts up to that point. Luckily, it doesn't work that way.

You can miss a day during the habit-forming process and still be on track.

If you slip up, your brain won't hit "reset" on the progress you've made. The neural pathway doesn't immediately vanish or even begin to reverse. It takes time to both fully form and fully unform habits, which is good news for your new habits!

The Habit Highway

Your new habit will eventually become automatic thanks to neuroplasticity. When you repeat something, your brain strengthens the connections between nerve cells, making the habit easier and more automatic over time.

This picture shows that some habits have strong connections, some are forming, and some don't have any form yet—they're just floating and ready to be connected.

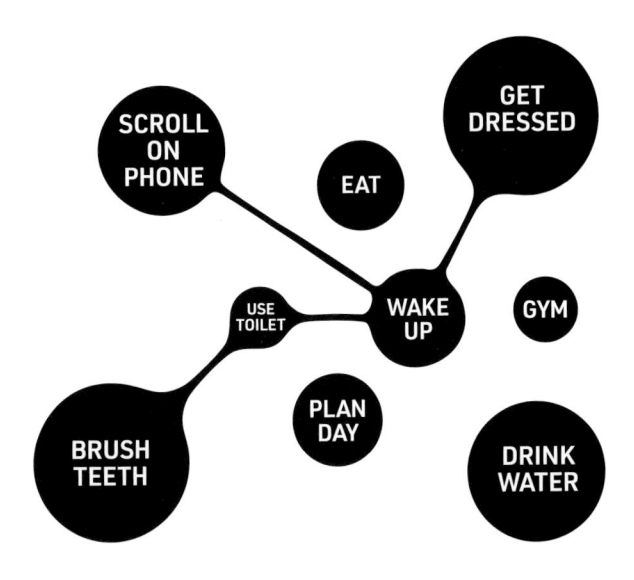

It's like building a smoother and faster highway for your habits in your brain. Each time you do it, you lay down another bit of the road.

→ WRITE IT DOWN: What Are Your Automatic Habits?

Write down the question: What do I already do without thinking about it? Then list your answers. Here are some examples of my automatic habits:

- Driving (I don't think, "I need to put the indicator on and turn my wheels.")
- Pick up my phone to check notifications
- Go to the bathroom as soon as I wake up
- Put hand cream on every night in bed
- Sit in the kitchen to eat breakfast
- Clean the kitchen every morning

This may seem silly to note these seemingly small details, but these are your preexisting habits, and we are about to use them as your foundations to build new habit highways!

Stack Your Habits to Form Them Fast

Now that you have your list of automatic habits, we are going to habit stack! Habit stacking is when you take a preexisting habit and do another habit at the same time or use the existing habit as a cue for the new habit.

Let's say that the new habit you want is to listen to audiobooks. You can look at your current automatic habits and see where you can habit stack this new one. From the examples I gave above, I can use driving. I already do so many automatic things here after my cue of getting in the car. I put my bag down, put my seat belt on, choose music on the radio, and everything that driving itself entails!

All I have to do is add in putting on an audiobook as I get in the car.

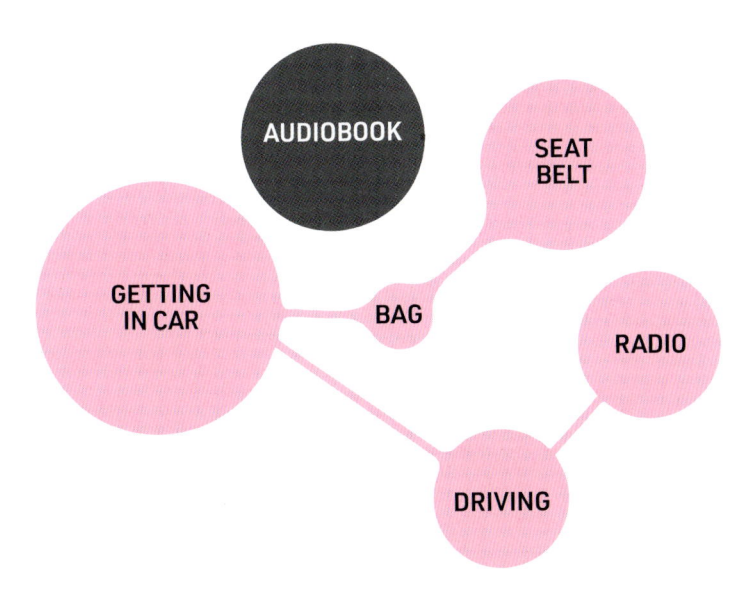

Eventually, as I repeat this new stacked habit, playing an audiobook becomes connected and automatic, and choosing music on the radio becomes redundant.

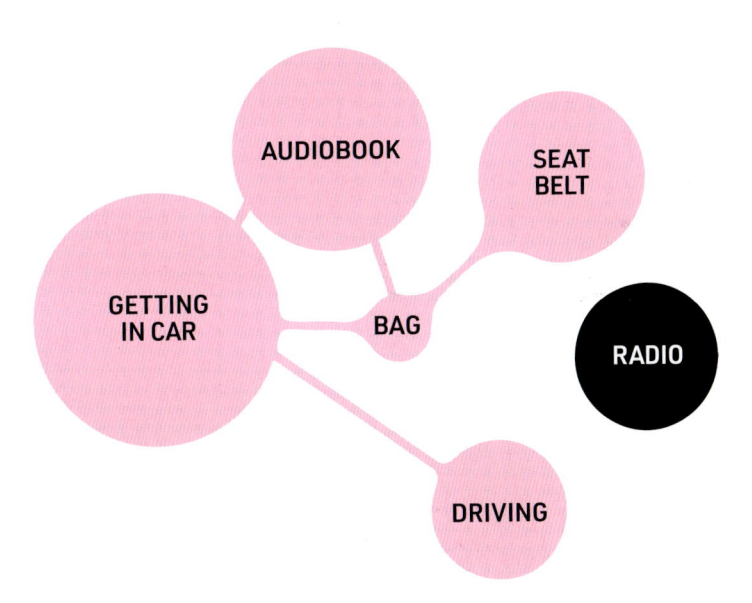

Habit stacking can be applied to all areas of your life. My nighttime routine used to consist of brushing my teeth then slumping in bed and scrolling on my phone until I passed out. Now I've built in so many healthy nighttime routine habits that all stem from this simple act!

Using brushing my teeth as the cue, I now wash my face (a three-step facial regime!), apply hand cream, spray on my topical magnesium supplement, brush my hair, plan the next day in my planner, sometimes scroll socials, and then play a sleep hypnosis audio to go to sleep. I'm aiming to have a phone-free space in my bedroom, but I am still in the habit forming and unforming process of this one!

Cues and Triggers

Sometimes you need to create a cue to trigger yourself into a new habit, even if you have stacked it next to an existing automatic habit! For example, if I'd already gone to the bathroom and brushed my teeth before bed, I would still forget to wash my face, so relying on an existing habit as the cue wasn't enough. I decided to create a new cue by displaying my face care products instead of leaving them in a drawer, so I was visually reminded to wash my face while I was in the bathroom. It can be as easy as that!

Here are some examples of *visual environment triggers*:

- Keep a daily planner near the bed (if evening planning).
- Put a daily planner where you eat breakfast (if morning planning).
- Leave a book on the side of your bed for evening reading.
- Keep night cream out of the draw and on your bedside table.
- Place supplements on display on the kitchen counter.
- Put a coaster on your desk at work to cue you to stay hydrated.
- Place a sticky note with the habit reminder in the area you carry out the new habit.

For habits that are time bound, such as attending a gym class or taking medication at a certain time, you can habit stack them with an existing activity, use visual cues, *and* add in reminders such as calendar alerts and alarm clocks. You can also prep the night before for habits such as a morning walk, workout, or healthy eating. For instance, I lay out my workout clothes in the evening to help me maintain a daily workout routine. By habit stacking this into my evening routine, I create a visual cue that triggers the time-bound habit.

Reveal Your Hidden Habits

An easy mistake to make when considering new habits that you want to form is to simplify them in your mind. How many times do you say something like "I'm going to go to the gym tomorrow," and then tomorrow comes and you forgot to set your alarm, you don't have any clean gym clothes, and the habit has fallen through before you've even been able to properly try!

That's because within some habits there are hidden habits! This is exactly why when we approach forming a new habit, we need to plan it well. That's where the blueprint comes in.

Use a Blueprint to Plan Your Habits

Below is the blueprint to habit planning. I have added in an example answer or explanation for each prompt. Copy this down and use the template whenever you want to begin forming a new habit:

My new habit: Thirty-minute daily walk
What can I stack this new habit next to? Getting dressed in the morning.
What new cues do I need to create for this habit? Visual cue of clothes and a digital reminder.
Are there any hidden habits within it? Setting the daily alarm/reminder; drinking my breakfast smoothie on the walk, so I need a clean to-go bottle. Night prep!

And just like with everything in an ADHDer's life, you *must* always ask yourself:

How can I make this easier? Listening to motivational music as I get ready and go for the walk!

SMARTER Goals

SMART goals are well known, but I have made them SMARTER for the ADHD community! What does it stand for?

Specific
Measurable
Achievable
Relevant
Time bound
Easy
Reveal the hidden habits!

Let me break it down for you so it makes sense and feels as easy as it is!

Make the goal *specific*: "Get healthy" as a new goal is too broad, and you won't know when you have achieved your goal with something this open to interpretation. Here is an example of a *specific* new goal: Start working out every day at the gym and increase water to two bottles a day.

How are you going to *measure* the success of the goal? New measurable goal: I will exercise for no less than thirty minutes a day and measure this on my fitness watch. Use a refillable water bottle and refill it twice per day.

Is your goal *achievable* and realistic? New achievable goal: Start working out at the gym twice a week for the first two weeks, and then increase each week until I do two gym workouts and two at-home workouts for thirty minutes. Increase water by one extra glass a day for a week before adding another glass until I have reached two liters.

Is your goal *relevant* to a bigger mission you have? Yes! I want to be able to run a marathon one day!

Make your goal *time bound*. I will do this for twelve weeks before reviewing and resetting.

Is the goal as easy as it can be? Make the goal easy: Workout three times a week for thirty minutes at home, outside, or at the gym. Use a water bottle to measure water intake and drink a minimum of one bottle a day. You can even reduce how long the goal lasts so that you can make it more challenging each week. The aim is to get you to begin the goal and to stick with it. The harder it is, the more resistance you will feel. Easier goals lead to bigger changes!

***Reveal* the hidden habits!** This is where you list all the new habits the goal requires and plan for them. For example:

- Wake up earlier.
- Set new alarms and reminders.
- Plan when to go to the gym each week.
- Track my water intake.
- Wash my gym clothes often.

Remember, overcommitting and telling yourself unnecessary lies lead to disappointment. So always be realistic and honest with yourself. If you need to make things easier, reduce goals down before you build up. Or you can add one new little habit at a time—that is more than okay! You always want to create opportunities to be proud of yourself and continue building on your self-trust and confidence.

→ FIVE-MINUTE RESET: Be Present

You have been thinking ahead throughout this entire chapter. Bring yourself back to the now with this reset exercise before moving on to the next chapter.

1. Take your hands and place them on your legs. Apply pressure for ten seconds. Notice that you are in control of this pressure as you count, and you can release at any time.
2. When you lift your hands from your legs, notice how light your hands and legs feel. How nice it is to release the pressure.
3. Sit for a moment feeling light after the release.

All this talk of change may trigger a little overwhelm, but this is often because we lack the belief that we can achieve what we desire. In the next chapter, we'll overcome this and switch on your manifesting mindset! It's time to live your dream life!

The Most Important Things You Need to Know

- Habits can take up to 254 days to fully form with an average of 66 days. So be patient with yourself.
- You can miss a day during the habit-forming process without the efforts being reversed.
- The habit loop consists of three key components: the *cue* or *craving*, the *response*, and the *reward*.
- Habit stacking is when you take a preexisting habit and do another habit at the same time or use the existing habit as a cue for the new habit.
- SMARTER goals stands for **S**pecific, **M**easurable, **A**chievable, **R**elevant, **T**ime bound, **E**asy, **R**eveal the hidden habits!

Manifesting Mindset:
Believe It to Achieve It!

IT MAY SEEM A LITTLE ODD to include a chapter on manifestation in a book about ADHD, but the goal of this book is to help you reset your perspective about what it means to have ADHD. With all the introspective healing and mindset shifts you have done, I am hoping that by now you can see that ADHD makes you magical! Now is the time to help you cultivate a manifesting mindset. Believe me, every ADHD client I have worked with is a natural manifester!

I have watched clients go from holding on tight to their ADHD label as a shield that blocks them from their dreams to adopting a manifesting go-getter attitude and using ADHD to propel them into their dream life.

For manifestation beginners, I like to give two explanations: the woo-woo magical version, and the more scientific, mindset-focused version.

Woo-Woo Magical Version

Manifestation is the process of turning your desires into reality by aligning your energy with what you want to attract. It's based on the idea that everything in the universe, including your thoughts, has a vibrational frequency. When you focus on positive intentions and visualize your goals, you raise your vibration to match the frequency of what you want to manifest. This creates a magnetic pull between you and your desires, allowing opportunities, people, and circumstances to align in your favor.

Scientific Growth-Mindset Version

Manifestation is the practice of using a positive growth mindset to influence your thoughts, emotions, and actions, which ultimately shape your reality. It's based on the psychological principle that our thoughts directly affect how we feel and act.

When you focus on a goal, your brain becomes primed to notice opportunities, and you gravitate to having a growth mindset. By setting clear intentions, visualizing success, and taking consistent actions, you create a feedback loop where your thoughts influence your actions, which then shape your environment. The result? You manifest real-world changes through deliberate focus, persistence, and self-improvement.

Merging Magic and Science: Energetic Communication

Now I am going to merge the worlds of magic and science by telling you about stress contagion. This is when you absorb stress from another person even without direct communication. Stress contagion can occur through subtle social cues and pheromones but also through, most interestingly, biomechanical rhythms. This is when you become stressed due to another person's increased heart rate, which forms *energetic communication*! This is one tiny snippet of science that proves we are energetic beings. The woo-woo explanation doesn't sound so out of this world now, huh?

Find Clarity and Dream Big!

Before I was able to manifest anything into my life, I had to become very clear about what it was I wanted to draw in. Just as you have to get SMARTER (Specific, Measurable, Achievable, Relevant, Time-Bound, Easy, Reveal the hidden habits) with your goals, you have to be very *specific* with what you desire too. This is often the first stumbling block. People are either too broad with what they are trying to manifest ("I want money") or they aren't sure about what they want. Instead of having a clear vision that triggers confident, driven energy, they feel uncertain and project that uncertainty outward. So, let's get crystal clear!

→ WRITE IT DOWN: Your Detailed Dreams

These questions are designed to help you gain clarity and tap into your innate desires, whether you have no idea what you want your future to look like or you just need to refine the details of your dream. These questions work for everyone, no matter where you are on your journey. (My answers are below if you need some examples.)

1. If the answer was "Yes! You can have that right now!" what would you ask for? (Exclude money from your answer for a more insightful reveal of what you truly crave from life.)
2. If everyone got paid the exact same amount, what career would you be drawn to now that money isn't the only incentive?
3. What activity makes you lose track of time because you get so into it?
4. What conversational topics make you excitable and talk quicker because you have so much you want to say?
5. What world problems do you feel passionate about solving?
6. What do you regret not pursuing so far and why?
7. Do you have a secret dream that has felt too impossible to share or attempt?
8. Who or what triggers jealousy in you? Why? What do they have that you desire?
9. Think of a time you have said or thought, "I wish I could do that." What was it?
10. How would you like to be remembered? It can help to imagine leaving behind a highlight reel of your past, present, and future life.

When I did this for myself years ago, I revealed to myself that . . .

1. I would ask for a loving, loyal partner and a beautiful home that feels secure.
2. I would choose writing books and creating videos as a career.
3. I lose all track of time when I write.
4. I get extremely excited when talking about how people's minds work!
5. I want to reduce mental health suffering and animal suffering.
6. I regret not pursuing a life-coaching career when I first said I wanted to at the age of eighteen! (I needed to live more, of course, but the qualifications would have been handy to have earlier!)
7. I had a secret dream of being known for something bigger than myself—for helping and changing the world somehow in a positive way.
8. I got jealous when I saw coaches publicly speaking and transforming people's lives.
9. I would often say, "I wish I could do that," when I saw others hosting TV documentaries.
10. I'd like to be remembered for helping others find happiness and having a positive chain reaction—inspired people inspire others!

As you are literally reading my book, you can see that my answers truly shaped my life. I developed and answered these questions after a messy breakup, when I sold my first home and moved back with my parents after I closed my first business due to stress. I did not know where or what to turn to!

I could see from my answers that I long for security and love to create. I have a natural yearning to write, I crave helping others and making positive change in the world, and I desire to share everything I learn.

ADHD Magic!
What Makes You a Natural Manifester?

Strong imagination: ADHDers have vivid imaginations, and they can create detailed mental pictures of their goals, which is a key for manifestation.

Passionate focus: When something excites you, you can hyperfocus, pouring all your energy into making your vision a reality, which drives manifestation forward.

Optimism and resilience: Many with ADHD have an innate optimism and bounce back quickly from setbacks, which helps them stay motivated and keep manifesting despite obstacles.

Quick adaptability: You are naturally adaptable, able to adjust your plans or vision when things don't go as expected, which helps you stay aligned with your manifestation goals.

Dream driven: The ADHD mind is often fueled by dreams and big ideas, making you naturally inclined to set ambitious goals, an essential part of manifesting a successful future.

Wing-it attitude: This is my favorite natural manifesting trait! You know that things just seem to work out if you need them to. A last-minute deadline—no biggie; you'll get it done. A job interview for a role that you don't actually have all the skills for—no problem; they will love your can-do attitude!

I did a social media post about exactly this, and the outrageously successful Paris Hilton liked and commented with emoji wings and hearts to show her full agreement on how having an ADHD wing-it attitude makes us natural manifesters!

Since I figured this out, I have grown a large social following where I create and support others every day. I have worked with and cofounded animal liberation charities and good cause businesses. I have studied and continue to study all things mental health and coaching related, and I am an ADHD coach and author! The one thing I know I still need to go after is producing and presenting a documentary . . . watch this space!

When you combine this practice with a manifesting growth mindset and a big dollop of ADHD go-getter energy, you are unstoppable!

Visualize Your Dreams into Your Reality: See It, Believe It, Achieve It

You know the old saying "You have to see it to believe it"? Well, we're going to switch this up a little bit by getting you to see it in your mind, fully believe in it, and achieve it! Remember, your subconscious mind absorbs everything as fact, so let's begin to feed it with excitement and success! Here are some of my favorite visualization practices.

Vision Board

I have made pictures from my vision board practically jump out of the frame and become my real-life reality! From my dream wedding, a houseboat, and a house with a view, to a book deal and social followers—everything in my current life was once an image I looked at on my vision board.

You can do it too. The first step is to choose images that closely resemble what you want, or make exact images by putting yourself in them! Sounds difficult, but the magic of AI has now made this incredibly easy. I was doing this way before AI by using the design tool Canva:

1. Click "Create Design" and select your image size.
2. Upload the images you have saved from the internet, such as your dream style of house, or search their stock images to use.
3. Upload an image of yourself and remove the background.
4. Adjust the size and position of yourself in the image.
5. Save!

Try to make the images as realistic as possible. The aim here is to trick your subconscious and trigger excited, high-energy emotions when you look at them.

Imagine Your Perfect Day

Get comfortable and imagine your perfect day. Don't worry about the concept of time or how the day fits together as you do this. Just let yourself flow through different aspects of what your perfect day would include, and be sure to add in what you desire to manifest.

I recommend that you practice imagining your perfect day just before sleep or first thing in the morning, when your brain waves are in a slower alpha or theta state. This means your conscious mind is less active and won't try to resist the information, and your subconscious mind is easier to access! When you're tired, your subconscious is at its most suggestible state, allowing your perfect-day manifestation to sink deeper and be accepted as truth.

Be Patient as You Build Your Visualization Practice

You may find that the first time you practice visualization, you don't get a clear image of the house you want to live in, the vacation you want to take, or the partner you want to have. Some details may feel blurred or be unclear. Instead of getting frustrated, think of this as a world-building exercise. You're creating a new world, like fantasy-book authors do.

Each time you do the visualization practice, you will build on the details that make it feel smooth and more vivid. Over time, the once-blurred edges will sharpen and the space will start to feel real, like stepping into a world you're crafting with each session. Just like an author shaping a universe, you're creating the blueprint for your future.

Visualize Specific Scenes to Energy-Match Your Manifestations

This is for specific desires you have, such as "a better car," and turning them into detailed visualized scenes. Visualizing your perfect day is great, but visualizing specific scenes will help you get there, one visualization at a time. The idea is to match the *exact* unique energy you have for each individual desire.

1. Decide on three future scenes you want to happen, such as getting a promotion, buying the house you desire, or finding the perfect partner.
2. Close your eyes and go to scene one. Watch yourself experiencing the moment and see how happy you are.
3. Notice the high energy and feel it in your body!

Repeat for all three scenes.

Notice Magical Moments to Reinforce Your Manifestation Mission

You can start practicing manifestation by paying attention to the mini magical moments in your day-to-day life. These are the small wins or synchronicities that show you're on the right path. For example, you might think of an old friend, then they text you out of the blue. Or you could be worrying about a problem and the solution suddenly presents itself in an unexpected way. Even finding a parking spot right when you need it or stumbling upon the perfect item you've been wanting on sale can be seen as tiny manifestations in action. By noticing and appreciating these little moments, you'll strengthen your ability to manifest even bigger things!

Start Small to Achieve Big!

When you start to practice manifestation, it can feel a little bit unrealistic. After all, you're used to trying to achieve things one way and now I'm asking you to use energy, imagery, and emotions. You may wonder, "Is it going to work?"

It's easy for me to say a huge YES! I manifested a house when we didn't even have the money for a deposit! But I built up to that. In the beginning, I needed the evidence of this actually working. I started small by noticing and changing the way in which I spoke about what I desired.

Start Small by Changing Your Language!

Just as you shifted the language you use around tasks from heavy language (got to, need to, have to) to light language (get to, want to, I am going to), you're going to shift your language around what you want to manifest. You want to move from disowning language to ownership language. Here are some examples and swaps to make:

Disowning Language	Ownership Language
"I can't afford that."	"That's for me!"
"I can't do that."	"If they can, I can."
"I don't know how."	"I can learn anything."
"I'll never be able to."	"I will make it happen."
"I wish I could."	"I'll find a way."
"It's impossible!"	"I'm figuring this out."
"I just can't seem to . . ."	"I will learn from whatever happens."
"I'll probably fail."	"I'm on my way to achieving it."
"I want."	"It's a fact that I'll make that happen!"

The last is my favorite because it takes full ownership and translates your desire into a future certain reality. I lost count of how many times I said, "It's a fact I will have my own book on my bookshelf!"

Start Small by Manifesting a Low-Value Item

All of us can have limiting money beliefs, so it can be hard to start with big-value mani-festations such as a car or house. So, it's easier to start by manifesting something that is less expensive and more doable. It's common practice in the law-of-attraction world to begin by trying to manifest seeing a butterfly, bee, or feather or finding a dollar bill on a certain day.

Once you have done this, it gives you a big boost of confidence to go after your bigger goals!

Revisit Your Limiting Beliefs

Now that you have become crystal clear about what it is you truly desire, new limiting beliefs may bubble to the surface.

In chapter 6, I guided you through how to pinpoint your limiting beliefs by exploring your "I am" statements, disprove the limiting beliefs with a "fact over fiction" practice, and then abolish them! Here is an example:

"I am never going to get that house!"

Ask yourself, "Who or what made me feel this way for the very first time?" This helps you detach from the belief being yours. Then move on to the practices that prove this belief to be untrue.

Revisit these steps for any limiting beliefs that arise as you yourself rise up and manifest your dream life!

→ WRITE IT DOWN: Must-Do Manifestation Exercise—Projected Gratitude

In chapter 5, I taught you how to cultivate gratitude and explained how to improve your written gratitude practice by adding details and avoiding lifeless bullet points!

Now we are going to expand on this to transform your gratitude practice into a magical manifestation must-do!

Start by doing your usual detailed gratitude practice. Fo example:

> I am so grateful for my cozy home. I always feel extremely safe in it. It keeps me warm when it's cold outside and protects me from the wind and rain. I love how I have decorated my bedroom and how calming it is to relax here. I'm really excited to decorate the living room next! I'm so lucky to have my own space. I am so thankful.

Write several things you are grateful for as you normally would, but add in projected gratitude for the new goals that you're manifesting. For this version, you'll write down something that you are manifesting, as if you already have it and you are already feeling grateful for it! For example:

> I am so grateful to experience producing and presenting my own documentary. It has been a life-changing experience, and I feel honored to have been able to interview so many interesting people and raise the awareness of ADHD! Yesterday was my absolute favorite day so far! I am so, so grateful and proud to be doing this.

Reread your gratitude entries for that day. When you do, you'll feel the gratitude as if it's real and feel as much thanks and joy as the achieved gratitudes you wrote. They all feel real to you!

This is my absolute fail-proof practice. Believe it or not, the night before a publishing house contacted me for the first time, I wrote the following projected gratitude in my journal:

> Thank you so much for my book publisher and the support I have in writing my book! I am so grateful to have a book deal and to be able to help so many people!

The next day I woke up to an email from the publishing house. At the risk of sounding somewhat insane, I shared my gratitude practice in my email back to her as I gleefully agreed to jump on a call! Luckily my editor, Jill, was just as wonderfully woo-woo and loved the synchronicity!

When you begin to successfully manifest in this way, you will feel truly magical, but this magic has always lived inside of you. You were never broken. The next and final chapter will officially reset your perspective of ADHD and guide you toward fully committing to your new life beyond these pages!

The Most Important Things You Need to Know

- Manifestation is the process of turning your desires into reality by aligning your energy with what you want to attract.
- Manifestation is the practice of using a positive-growth mindset to influence your thoughts, emotions, and actions, which ultimately shape your reality.
- There are many scientific findings that prove that we are energetic beings.
- Start small by manifesting a "low-value" item, such as a dollar bill, bee, or butterfly.
- Use visualization to manifest: see it, believe it, achieve it.
- Revisit chapter 6 to overcome any limiting beliefs that arise.
- Start to switch your language from *disowning language* to *ownership language*.
- Use the Must-Do Manifestation Exercise—Projected Gratitude.

You Got This!
Preparing for Your Life Beyond These Pages

BEFORE YOU HEAD OUT TO CHASE YOUR DREAMS and live your best ADHD life, I want to remind you that your ADHD is *exactly* what makes you magical. You were never broken—just a little unmanaged and misunderstood, both by others and maybe even yourself at times. But now? Now you're stepping into your full power.

To give you a little extra boost of confidence, here's the newly improved, not-so-official ADHD "symptoms" list (because let's face it, the old one needed an upgrade!):

WHY YOU'RE *SO* MAGICAL LIST

- **Limitless creativity:** Your ideas never stop flowing. If there's a box, you don't just think outside it—you turn it into a rocket ship!
- **Happy when hyperfocusing:** When something grabs your attention, you're unstoppable. Who needs sleep when you've got a passion project in front of you?
- **Master multitasker:** Who else can be brainstorming, eating lunch, texting three friends, and planning next week's world takeover . . . all at the same time?
- **Problem-solving ain't your problem:** Challenges? You eat them for breakfast! Your brain is wired to think up creative solutions that others miss. You're always three steps ahead.
- **Endless energy:** Forget regular pace. Your mind is wired for 2X speed!

- **The most curious of cats:** Your need to hunt for new things to do and learn is what keeps life exciting!
- **Big-hearted empath:** You feel everything deeply, which makes you not only a good friend but also someone who understands people like nobody else.
- **Adventure seeker:** You crave excitement, and that means your life is never boring. It's a wild, wonderful ride!
- **Social bumblebee:** Skip the small talk. Spill your deepest desires! You want to feel it all, connect quickly, and uncontrollably laugh like you've been besties for a decade!
- **Risk-taker:** Playing it safe? Not your style! You thrive on bold moves and taking chances that leave others in awe of your bravery and determination.
- **Born boss:** You naturally lead, thrive in chaos, and think outside the box. Basically the perfect combo for launching and running your own empire!
- **Natural manifester:** You're not just a daydreamer. You're a dream *maker*.

So next time someone tries to hit you with the old-school ADHD "symptoms," just smile and hand them *this* list. You're not just living with ADHD—you're thriving because of it!

→ WRITE IT DOWN: Symptoms That Sparkle

Here is your final reframing practice to fully finalize your ADHD reset!

In your journal, write down the "symptoms" that have helped you so far and will help you achieve your dreams going forward. Describe how they set you apart from others and have even been envied by others! You can do this as a free-flowing journal entry or in sections. Make sure to write as many symptoms as you can think of and be detailed in why they benefit you! Here is a short version:

Symptoms that have helped me: I am really adaptable, and this helped me when I worked for a small business and had to wear many hats. Without being adaptable, I wouldn't have gained so much varied experience and been able to apply and get the job I have today!

Symptoms that will help me achieve my dreams: I dare to take risks, and I'm going to need to bet on myself when I start my business.

Symptoms others envy: My best friend always says she can't believe how much I can juggle and wishes she could throw herself at as many things as I do!

Then to complete the reframe and full ADHD reset, finish the journal practice with how grateful you are to have all those wonderful ADHD "symptoms." For example:

> I can't imagine not having those traits and not being able to do all those things. I love that I can, and I'm so grateful for every single one of them!

Finalize this exercise with the following sentence:

> ADHD is my greatest strength!

The Promise: Living Your Dream Life

At the beginning of the book, I asked you to make a commitment to read it to the end, and you are very nearly there! (Remember to celebrate yourself for this achievement!). Now I am going to ask you to do the exact same thing when it comes to your dream life. After all, you have proven to yourself that you can stay committed. Now you know that when you make a clear commitment and have a burning desire to become the best version of yourself, your success is inevitable!

Success means different things to different people, and so does *dream life*. To some, their dream life is fancy cars and a big house; to others, it solely focuses on their mental health and overall happiness. Whatever *dream life* means to you, you can have it if you put the teachings of this book into practice—because you have learned it all!

You know how to heal, reframe, and make peace. You can dispute limiting beliefs and move past them. You can rewire your mind to think better thoughts, feel better feelings, and positively influence your daily reality. You can treat yourself better—with love, compassion, and kindness. You know how to navigate and overcome the more troublesome aspects of having ADHD and know how to manage the once unmanageable. You know you absolutely can create better habits, achieve bigger goals, and go after whatever dream you desire! Whatever it is, you can do it now!

The nonnegotiable to include in your dream life is to stay committed to maintaining your increased self-love, compassion, and kindness and newfound appreciation of having ADHD.

Say the words: "I promise to live my dream life!"

→ WRITE IT DOWN: Dream to Reality

Just like you did at the start of the book, write down *why* you are going to create your dream life. Visualize the outcome of sticking to your promise! This is your why! Embody every positive emotion you will feel in your new reality: Excited! Fulfilled! Proud, happy, content, finally at peace. Give yourself a sense of the reward you will get and reconfirm your commitment to live your dream life. For example:

> I promise to live my dream life because . . . I am done with wishing to be like someone else. I want to be the person who makes me proud! I deserve to be happy. I deserve to wake up and feel excited about what it is I am doing that day. I love myself just like I love my best friend, and I want to be as happy and fulfilled as possible. I promise to do everything possible to live my dream life!

Now add specific details about what your dream life looks like. Start with the words:

> My dream life will look like . . .

Then finish it with:

> This dream is a future reality because I have made this promise to myself.

ADHD Reset Integration

Now that you have made this promise to yourself, visualize the future you! Close your eyes and feel what it feels like to be there. This is the version of you that has kept this promise and maintained your new positive perspective about having ADHD. Feel how powerful you are—accomplished, confident, secure, and happy!

Once you feel you are embodying your promise-keeping future self who has it all, write a letter as your future self to you now. Give yourself praise, feedback about how you kept your promise, encouragement—whatever you need your future self to say to you now. Say it! You are embodying yourself and raising your energy to that of your higher-self! For example:

> I am so proud of you for making that promise to yourself. This is the most life-changing promise you have ever made. I am so happy now, and it is all thanks to you. You still have tough moments and even days, but now that you have the tools, they just don't hold you back like before! You manage it and you maintain your positive outlook on your life. You achieve everything and so much more than you promised to yourself . . .

You've Got This!

I stared at the blinking cursor, just sitting there, waiting for me to find the perfect words to leave you with. Words that would make you feel motivated, inspired, and strong enough to live your best life after you finish this book. Then I realized . . . you will always have it!

This book isn't like a story that you read once and can never experience the same way again. It's here for you as many times as you need it. The practices can be repeated to find new revelations, the information can be more easily absorbed when it feels most relevant to you.

You can use the advice to better support you during a day of struggle or tap into the motivational magic to shine even brighter on days when you feel energized and unstoppable. This book can be your gentle reminder on the tough days or a big push when you're going after your goals!

Don't ever be afraid to come back to these pages when you need to.

But for now, acknowledge that you did read *The ADHD Reset* and are beginning to do the work that will change your life for the better!

☐ Completed *The ADHD Reset*

Remember, you've got this book for whenever you need to reset yourself.

And remember that you now have a newfound understanding and perspective of ADHD, a reset that empowers you to embrace and love your differences.

Now go out there and get the life you deserve. I'm so proud of you, and I'm with you every step of the way, cheering you on.

ACKNOWLEDGMENTS

I WON'T SAVE THE BEST FOR LAST: my husband, Dr. Ross Hammond, truly deserves the top spot in my acknowledgments. Thank you, Ross, for being the person I counted on throughout the entire book-writing journey to check my work, check that I was sticking to tight deadlines, check that I'd eaten, check that I felt loved throughout, and (admittedly) check my sanity at times! Truly the list goes on, adding to all the reasons why I respect and love you. Thank you for being my person.

I'd like to thank my family and friends for being so understanding when I declined invites, canceled plans, took a few days too long to reply, and for letting me dine and dash while I became consumed with research and writing. I'm lucky to (still!) have you. I would especially like to thank my empowering grandma, Shirley Michalski, who has always believed in me and shaped many aspects of my positive mindset, including the power of the mind. An infinite thank-you to my admirably ambitious parents, Fay and Martin Michalski, who instilled self-belief and drive in me. Without you, Mum and Dad, I wouldn't have been able to receive my ADHD diagnosis when I did—a huge turning point in my life that has led to helping countless others. I want you to know how much impact your love, kindness, and generosity have on the world. Thank you.

I am incredibly grateful to the many mentors, coaches, and therapists who have supported me throughout life, helping me along my healing journey.

Thank you to the Quarto Group for believing in this project and helping me reach the ADHD community in a way I once dreamed of. Jill Alexander, Chrystle Fiedler, and Emily Wichland: Thank you for your understanding and willingness to provide extra and tailored support to navigate working with an ADHD author.

To every professional who has devoted their life to studying ADHD and sharing their work publicly—thank you! I lost hours reading your research but gained a world of understanding and respect.

Last but most certainly not least, to my social media community and every reader. *None of this would be possible without you.* I am forever grateful to each and every one of you. Every page reflects your support of my dream! Thank you for making it a reality. I hope I have returned the favor and helped you step toward your dream life too!

ABOUT THE AUTHOR

CLAIRE MICHALSKI, THE FOUNDER OF MODERN HIPPIE MINDSET, is a British mindset and ADHD coach, businesswoman, public speaker, and author. She is passionate about helping people with ADHD live more holistic, purpose-driven lives. After years of navigating her own ADHD challenges, Claire embraced it as a unique gift, creating a coaching methodology that blends scientific insights with holistic wellness practices. With a background in techniques like neurolinguistic programming (NLP), hypnotherapy, and motivational coaching, she empowers her clients to reframe their ADHD experience and unlock their full potential.

Claire shares free coaching content online, offering wellness advice and practical ADHD management tips through her social platforms that reach millions worldwide. Alongside her coaching and content creation, she has founded and worked with good-cause businesses and charities, furthering her mission of equality and positive impact.

With a background in event management, she plans to create *ADHD Reset* retreats, immersive wellness experiences aimed at helping participants reset and refocus in a supportive environment.

Through her courses, public speaking, one-on-one coaching, and community-driven initiatives, Claire helps others live focused, stress-free, and fulfilling lives rooted in personal growth and purpose. *The ADHD Reset* is her first book, based on the teachings she has successfully practiced with her clients. Learn more at modernhippiemindset.com.

INDEX

A

Actions
  affirmations and, 72
  beliefs and, 74, 80, 81
  emotions and triggering positive, 35, 38
  journaling about, 32-33
  masking and, 36
  self-sabotage and, 81-82
  thoughts as trigger for emotions and,
      60-61, 73
  See also Reflections and actions
Adaptability, masking compared to, 45, 46, 47-48
ADHD
  actors with, 47
  common misperceptions about, 61-62, 94
  common unmet needs of individuals with, 107
  depression as common diagnosis for
      those with, 26
  diagnosis of, 17-18
  genetic link, 147, 155
  magical "symptoms" of, 196-198
  See also Diagnosed ADHD; Undiagnosed ADHD
Adrenaline, 115
Affirmations
  actions and, 72
  examples of in-conversation, 92-93
  positive thinking and, 72
  power of projected, 91-92, 95
  as triggers, 91
  for wiring in positive beliefs, 84-85
American Journal of Psychiatry, 127
American Psychiatric Association, 124
Anderson, Linda, 32
Anxious-preoccupied attachments, 158, 159
Attachment styles, 158, 165

B

Being in the moment, practices for, 49
Beliefs
  actions and, 74, 80, 81
  affirmations for wiring in positive, 84-85
  conscious, 75
  core, 74
  feedback loops and strengthening of, 75-76
  formation of, 74, 76, 77
  self-sabotage and, 81
  subconscious, 75
  See also Limiting (subconscious) beliefs

Best-friend perspective
  as connection to higher self, 101
  described, 105
  importance of, 100-101
  in journaling, 56-57, 59, 102, 105
  self-love and, 59
Blueprint to plan habits, 183
Body doubling, 32
Boredom and brain, 121
Boundaries
  described, 112
  effect of having poor, 98
  self-worth, 112, 113
  setting, 113, 162
Brain
  activation of mirror neurons, 38
  boredom and, 121
  default-mode network, 122
  ditching negative stimulation of, 122-123
  effect of negative information on, 77
  flooding of, with negative emotions, 126, 133,
      139-140
  hormonal response to stress in, 114, 123
  during hypnosis, 86
  negative self-boosting and, 118
  neural pathways in, 66
  neuroplasticity of, 179-180
  organizing, for task completion, 169-170
  positive self-boosting and, 119-121
  RDS and, 148
  right side of, 6, 27
  training with thoughts, 60
  triggering executive function circuits, 173, 175
  See also Dopamine

C

CHADD (Children and Adults with
      Attention-Deficit/Hyperactivity Disorder),
      26
Chaos
  cause of, 157
  comfortableness with, 116, 123
  dopamine and, 115-117
  emotional dysregulation and dysregulated
      nervous system and, 130, 133
  relationships and, 157
Cognitive reappraisal, 127
Cold-water therapy, 120, 132

reading this book: obstacles to, 9
relationship with self, 99
reparenting inner teenager, 110–111
taking medications, 19
tapping into desires, 188–189
things curious about, 23
unmasking ADHD, 44–45, 48
using reframing technique, 57–58, 59
Jung, Carl, 51

L

Language
for manifestations, 192–193, 195
for self-talk, 168, 175
Leaf, Caroline, 27, 28
Lewis, Andrew, 27
Light language, 168, 175
Limiting (subconscious) beliefs
acceptance of, 76–78
described, 75
difficulty of changing, 79
feedback loops and, 80
feeling badly from, 80
journaling to pinpoint, 83–85
manifestations and, 193–194
need for, 76
negative statements about self, 53
as protection, 78
shadow work and, 53
triggering of emotions and actions by, 80, 85
using hypnosis to replace limiting,
    with positive, 87–90
voicing, 90–91
Love bombing, 157

M

Management tools, 167
Manifestations
basic facts about, 186–187, 195
characteristics making individual
    natural for, 189
expanding gratitude practice into, 194–195
language for, 192–193, 195
limiting beliefs and, 193–194
practicing, 192, 193, 195
visualizations matching, 191, 195
Masking
actions and, 36
adaptability compared to, 45, 46, 47–48
basic facts about, 36
benefits of, 52
burnout from, 42–43
emotional dysregulation and, 127
fear of being found out and, 41

fitting in and, 38, 39, 40
four common behaviors, 37
imposter syndrome and, 42
magic of ADHD and, 39
mirroring compared to, 46
perfectionism and, 41
at work, 40–41
McCabe, Jessica, 152
Media consumption and negative thoughts, 68
Medications, decision to take, 19–20
Men, common shadow for, 50
Mental energy, habitual thoughts and, 66
Mental health versus physical health, 63
Mind reading, 38
Mirroring
described, 46, 49
feeling different and, 38
masking and, 46
Mood music, 120–122
Music, 120–122

N

Naturopathic remedies, 132
Negative self-boosting, 118–119, 123
Neuroplasticity, 179–180
Neuropsychiatric Disease and Treatment, 147
Noradrenaline, 115

O

1-2-3 move method, 175
Overcompensation, 41–42
Overpromising, 94, 95
Ownership language, 192–193, 195
OWNLY planners, 170

P

Pain, limiting beliefs and avoiding, 78
Parasympathetic nervous system, 34–35
People-pleasing
beginning of, 13
overcompensating and, 42
Perfectionism and masking, 41
Persona
benefits of, 52
described, 51, 52
survival and, 53
Physical health versus mental health, 63
Positive music, 121
Positive self-boosting, 119–121, 123
Positive self-talk, 91–93
Positive thinking, 65, 70–73
Predictability, limiting beliefs and, 78
Projected affirmations, power of, 91–92, 95
Psyche, Jung's model of, 51–53